DESIGNING

and

PLANNING CLOTHES

The principles of design illustrated
and explained in their practical appli‑
cation to correct dress for all types

Published by

Woman's Institute

of Domestic Arts and Sciences, Inc.

Scranton, Pa.

This Bramcost Publications edition is an unabridged republication
of the rare original work first published in 1925.

www.BramcostPublications.com

ISBN 10: 1-934268-70-4
ISBN 13: 978-1-934268-70-4

Library of Congress Control Number: 2008927794

Bramcost
Publications

CONTENTS

BECOMING ADEPT IN DESIGNING

Perfection Comes Through Knowledge of the Dress Essentials, Love of Beauty, and Interest and Pride in Personal Appearance

KNOWLEDGE OF DRESS ESSENTIALS

WOMEN, young, mature, or elderly, at home or in business, should always try to look their best, to be just as pleasingly dressed as possible; in fact, to be so correctly dressed as always to evidence good taste, for good taste, after all, is the only real authority in dress. Without it, dress loses all its power of charm or influence.

It is easy enough to say, "I design all my own clothes;" but to design them so that they are right in every detail for you means that you have studied definitely or that you are naturally gifted, or that, through a happy combination, you are both trained and gifted. And to design clothes that are correct means to design artistic clothes, an achievement worthy of pride.

Gaining Dress Knowledge.—With dress knowledge, like that of all other subjects, much more is involved than the foundation principles. For instance, we may learn to speak English correctly, but we can speak it more beautifully by increasing our vocabulary, by learning voice intonation, and by improving the subject of our conversation. And so we may learn the essential rules of dress, but unless we absorb them and try to grow by this means, we cannot expect a beautiful interpretation of dress.

The importance of practice cannot be overestimated. Just as a good cook perfects her cooking by practice, so a good dressmaker improves with each creation, provided her basic rules are correct and she knows the reason back of everything she does. But the desire to know—the incentive to gain by experiment and application is all important. So to be able to delight in truly artistic clothes, keep always the rules of design before you and try to carry them out so perfectly that no trace of them will be visible.

Whistler says, "A picture is finished when all trace of the means used to bring about the end has disappeared. To say of a picture, as is often said in its praise, that it shows great and earnest labor, is to say that it is incomplete and unfit for view." So work and practice; and when skill is acquired, forget the source of the rule, applying it as natural knowledge. That, in itself, makes perfection possible.

Purpose of Book.—This book of rules comes to start you thinking correctly in terms of lines, proportions, materials, colors, and their combinations as applied to yourself, and then to show you how to use all correctly in creating and making practical and beautiful clothes that will be an expression of your own individuality.

If clothes, beauty, harmony, and perfection do not interest you, you cannot expect success from this book. But if you do wish to learn, if you wish rules that are safe and that will aid you in expressing beauty and grace intelligently, then follow through these pages. You may find some rules that you already know, but at the same time you will find many truths and essentials that will prove forever helpful.

EXPRESSING BEAUTY IN DRESS

Love of beauty in dress is a heritage of woman. Since Nature provided her with lovely curves, delicate skin, and luxuriant hair, it seems right that she should express beauty, whatever her station in life. Beauty is not a perquisite of riches. Indeed, we as often see real beauty among the very poor as among the very rich, for exquisite fabrics are of very little consequence unless skin, hair, and eyes have in them enough loveliness of texture, color, or expression to harmonize with beautiful fabrics and accessories.

In this era of rapidly advancing civilization, when from all over the world come beautiful weaves, laces, jewels, and furs, a woman must be indifferent indeed who does not feel a definite desire to possess some of them. And the keener the appreciation, the more happy the interpretation. So if we are "thrilled" with lovely, fresh gingham, crisp lawn, and the sheen of silk, if the lure of lace follows us throughout the years, then we are good subjects to promote the crusade of beautiful, becoming, and appropriate dress.

INTEREST AND PRIDE IN APPEARANCE

Necessity for Interest.—To be practical and at the same time dress correctly, smartly, becomingly, distinctively—whichever you choose—you must develop to a high degree your interest in clothes, in materials, colors, and fashions, and "keep everlastingly at it."

Throughout all ages of human activity, interest has preceded success. No matter how insignificant the task or the thing, we must think about it, and, as some people say, actually "love it into being." We must be interested in our occupation to know all its virtues; and the undertaking, whatever it is, must command our respect so that in times of crises, when we see our interests in jeopardy, put into disfavor, or something else preferred to them, our courage will be stimulated in every fiber to prevent failure of that which we prize.

Breadth of achievement lies in the interest manifest. In every occupation, every business, every task, from mixing biscuits to winning great battles, interest always precedes success. A disinterested mind and heart never made an appetizing pan of biscuits, and it is certain no disinterested general ever led an army or idea to victory.

Without interest, work is tedious and slow of accomplishment; with it, work is done so quickly that we are reaching out all the while for more to do.

And that is the whole point of this discourse on dress designing. Don't consider study a punishment; don't struggle to make a dress. Rather, try to find a way to arouse your interest, to set it on fire; then you can realize all the pleasure of accomplishment and all the success that whole-hearted interest can produce.

And, most important of all, keep up your interest. This you can do if you work to learn by absorption rather than by injection; if you get all the fun possible out of making your dresses and hats; if you learn to make your clothes so that they will make you more attractive; if you dress yourself up a dozen times a day in your imagination. Then you will find that every design interests you, that every piece of cloth evidences possibilities, and that your fingers take on a new confidence, such as only interest can give.

Wholesome Pride.—Giving thought to one's dress is a delightful way to express beauty, and proper interest in such matters helps in keeping a woman young and interesting. Also, correct, womanly clothes, attractively worn, can give happiness not only to the woman herself but to her family and friends. But clothes are not all. A lovely dress can be belittled seriously if its owner has not enough pride in her personal appearance to make herself ready to don it. And how is she to do this? By dressing herself with precise care, giving as much attention to the preparation of her person, her bath, and her dash of powder as to the donning of the dress itself.

One woman, who looks like a fashion plate in the daytime and like a dream lady at night, always gets everything together on the bed before she starts to dress. She insists that it takes only a little longer to do this, that it saves time when she does get ready to dress, and that she is always better satisfied with the results. She says, "I know then that I have the right slip, the right stockings, that my gloves are suitable, and that there are no flaws that need attention. When laying my clothes out on the bed, I always make all the little repairs that are necessary and do all the brushing or freshening that is needed; then when I am ready to dress, I feel a sense of satisfaction that I can find in no other way."

And so should you, who are striving to express yourself more beautifully, to dress with more satisfaction and peace of mind, try this simple little plan of having sufficient pride in your appearance to think about what you are going to wear and to get it ready before you start to dress. Don't cheat yourself or those who must see you. Don't be dowdy. Life is too short and too real for that. Learn to be proud of yourself and dress so that you will feel a sense of security and assurance. A right hat, a right dress, correctly worn, can do wonders as a tonic. Try it. It is truly a good prescription. Thus, watching always what you see in your mirror, your fashion books, on the streets, and in the shops, you will find that which is appropriate, becoming, and wholly lovely for you.

Dress that is beautifully alluring and complimentary is woman's privilege, and any woman who allows her lack of knowledge of, or interest in, her clothes to make her unhappy or unpleasing to see has only herself to blame, for it doesn't take money to be well dressed, but information, ingenuity, energy, interest, and pride—and no woman wants to admit herself without any one of these.

DRESSING WITH APPROPRIATENESS

Considering Clothes with Respect to the Age, Mood, Inclination, and Temperament of the Wearer

For the serious mood, choose clothes that have conservative lines, are quiet in color, and are made of good materials, but are smart in every respect. Have the accessories of a corresponding nature.

PERIODS IN WOMAN'S DRESS

THERE are three periods in woman's dress, and every woman must be alert and ready to make the change as she grows out of one into the other. She should be eager to express to the best of her ability the essentials of these three periods.

The first, of course, is youth, the expression of which is vivaciousness. The second period begins where the first ends and is that of the woman from thirty to fifty, when her greatest assets are smartness and charm. The third period is that of the woman older than fifty, whose dress should express dignified comfort. In each case, however, women should dress as though they knew youth, as though it were just around the corner, but give evidence that they have so close a hold on charm and becomingness that youth is no longer essential.

THE "FRIENDLY" GOWN

In modern dress, a very definite change has come, even in the present generation. The Sunday dress, or outfit, disappeared along with the appearance of corset stays. Almost every one still has a best dress, but instead of one new or "good" dress a season, there are usually two or three or four, and they are all

different enough to allow the expression of ourselves, or our moods, in them.

Did you ever start to dress and feel that you just couldn't put on a green dress, but that the old blue one suited you without effort? There are many women who have had beautiful gowns made especially for certain formal occasions, yet who, when the hour came to don them, would put on a simple, friendly dress and wear it with the vague and somewhat unsatisfactory explanation that they just "didn't feel like wearing the new dress."

Sometimes we hear the question, "Where is the new dress you were going to wear today?" and hear, "Oh, I didn't want to feel all dressed up, so I wore this old dress." Is it modesty or mood, temperament or indifference? Perhaps the best explanation is that it is individuality, which, as a composite of mood, inclination, and temperament, is wholly understandable and allowable. *But*—and it is a big *but*—if you are sensitive to all three of these whims, watch your buying carefully. Don't go shopping when in a gay mood, for you are likely to come home with a burnt-orange chiffon velvet when a navy serge would have been much more useful and more satisfying. Of course, if you are one who can afford to have luxuri-

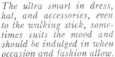

The ultra smart in dress, hat, and accessories, even to the walking stick, sometimes suits the mood and should be indulged in when occasion and fashion allow.

Simplicity should invariably be the keynote of the service dress. A whim of the season may be evident in such details as the collar and cuffs.

ously adorned closets, you need not be so cautious in selection, but all who must get full value from every dress must constantly watch what they buy so that it is suitable, wearable, and agreeable, and so that, after these essentials, it expresses as much beauty as possible.

INTELLIGENT EXPRESSION
OF IDEAS

In common with the rest of womankind, you have a vision of how you should look in a certain costume. You dream about it, buy it, work with it, wear it, and usually are not disappointed. But sometimes you feel as you do when you work very industriously to bake a lovely cake and discover, after it starts to bake, that you have left out the leavening. You must learn the rules of dress as definitely as those of cake making, so that the ingredients will all harmonize and produce, with your intelligent effort, something approaching perfection as well as expressive of you as an individual.

If you are earnest in your desire to evidence a correct expression of dress, you must work to overcome any consciousness of your own physical shortcomings. You should avoid discussing them just as you would the ailments of a child in the child's presence. You must work to be fair to yourself, to overcome as much as possible your physical deficiencies, and to enhance such beauty as you have with the choice of every fabric, design, or trimming that you use.

Curbing One's Preferences.—One's ideas of dress undergo a considerable change from time to time, though one naturally shows preference, even after having long outgrown them by years, size, and individuality, for the styles in which one was most attractive. To prove this, ask any group of women what style or period of dress they think most beautiful and what they would prefer to see return as the fashion. Invariably, you can trace their preferences to the type of dress that was favored when they were at the peak of their youth, beauty, and vivaciousness. This is a truly lovely sentiment, but oh, so dangerous, when one adores basques, for instance, and weighs one hundred and sixty, or flaring skirts and one's waist measures a good yard around.

Intelligent, self-denying sentiment is the only kind that should be allowed to influence a woman if she wishes to evidence a smart or becoming interpretation of the dress of the day. Because a sailor hat, a tunic skirt, a tight waist, or a long shoulder was once very becoming to a woman, is no reason at all why it should forever be, for as time passes she changes in build, in lines, in expression, in need, and in enthusiasm. Fabrics, colors, and lines also change so much that she must learn to blend them all intelligently, deftly, delightfully, if she would express that degree of artistic perfection that we all, as women of this enterprising day and age, should insist on and strive for—that perfection of which Whistler spoke, a perfection so subtly achieved as to appear wholly free of any means.

A woman passes through many periods of dress from youth to maturity. At times she can be piquant, other times vivacious, again dignified, alluring, or majestic. So every one of us must watch and see by what route, or as what type, we, as individuals, can best express the fashions, and then work for a perfect expression of that type.

For the gay mood, let your frock express delight in fabric and color, choosing from the brighter tones and the bouffant materials, if you are young, and from the rich, beautiful ones, if you are not.

SELF-ANALYSIS IN DRESS PLANNING

The Basis of All Improvement in Dress
Lies in Learning the Truth About Oneself

DETERMINING YOUR TYPE

THE first step toward improvement of any sort lies in determining definitely just where the need for improvement lies. Therefore, as a basis for your study of dress, take inventory of your good points and of your poor ones. Be fair with yourself, neither flattering nor cheating, for you cannot afford to be over-optimistic nor overpessimistic but must know the truth in order to make the desired improvement.

First recognize your size and build. Read carefully the chapter on "Line in Figure and Dress," as given in the volume, *Harmony in Dress*. Stand in front of a full-length mirror with a tape measure and a yard-stick, determining definitely the figure type you represent. Measure your bust, hips, waist, sleeve length, and neck. Also, measure around your figure over the arms, for some figures look stout or thin because of the arms, and a little consideration regarding these will help to lose the tendency to appear out of size.

Essential Points.—Are you stout or slender? Are you swayback, full in the abdomen, square or narrow of shoulders, or wide or narrow of hips? Determining all such points as these is essential to a right analysis of your individual problem.

The American figure changes from time to time, ranging from the sturdy to the petite, and then to the extreme slender. So we can hope that, at some time, there will recur the Venus figure, which artists have held for centuries as the perfect type. Certain it is that her measurements are more nearly in accord with the figure representing good health than are the measurements of the ideal modern type, whose figure is too slight to suggest perfect physical development.

After you have determined whether you can be cataloged in the small, the extreme slender, the slender, the full-proportioned, the stout, or the overstout class, consider the lines that are becoming to your type. The younger you are, the more severe the lines that you may wear; the older, the softer must be the lines; and in between, proportionately. If you are young and stout, be careful to dress so that you do not look too matronly, while if you are of the slender, mature type, use definite discretion in choosing design, fabric, and color in order not to appear too youthful.

Stout women must, of necessity, wear the best their purses can buy, for tawdry garments on large people are conspicuous. Such women must depend on fabrics to make up for the daintiness and lithesome-ness that they cannot manifest. This does not mean that the fabric must be elaborate, but it must be of good quality and in good taste. Small people, on the other hand, must not choose coarse, big-design fabrics.

Rating Yourself.—Score yourself on the points given in the table below and see where your need for improvement lies. Allow 10 points for each group, apportioning them among the various subheadings. For example, allowing 10 points for "size," apportion 3⅓ points to each of the three subheadings, "height," "weight," and "lines." If you are neither too short nor too tall, rate yourself 3⅓ points on "height," while if you are over or under normal height, reduce the points in ratio to the amount that you vary. Similarly, rate yourself as to the other divisions, finally adding the total number of points.

Then, whether it is high or low, start to improve each point on which you fall below the required rating and gradually work for a percentage that will be as near perfection as you can make it.

TABLE I

Points	Subdivisions	Rating
Size	Height; weight; lines	
Type	Coloring (skin, hair, eyes); age	
Cleanliness	Neatness; nature of skin	
Sense of Fitness	Idea of individual becoming-ness; of appropriateness	
Interest	Incentives for attractiveness	
Sewing Skill	Ability to design; to secure desired effects; technique	
Style Sense	Sense of line, color, smartness	
Buying Sense	Knowledge of fabrics and trimmings and their fash-ion value	
Wearing Clothes	Poise; grace; charm	
Decorative Value	General appearance; special features	

PRINCIPLES OF DESIGN

Successful Designing Depends on Proportion, Balance, and Proper Distribution of Light and Dark Areas

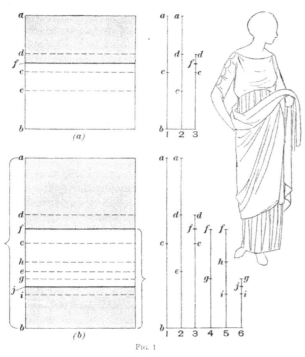

FIG. 1

given space, irregular divisions are less monotonous and far more pleasing to the eye than a number of sections of equal size.

For example, divide the given space, *ab*, view (*a*), Fig. 1, into halves, as indicated by the dotted line *c*, and then into thirds, as indicated by the dotted lines *d* and *e*; then divide in half the space between *c* and *d*, as indicated by the heavy line *f*. This line divides the space *ab* into two parts that form a more pleasing division than if it were divided exactly into halves, thirds, fourths, or into any equal division. The lines at the right show clearly the three steps in this operation.

As shown in view (*b*), the division can be carried much further. Divide the entire space *ab* in half, indicating the division by the dotted line *c*, and then into thirds, as indicated at *d* and *e*. Next, divide in

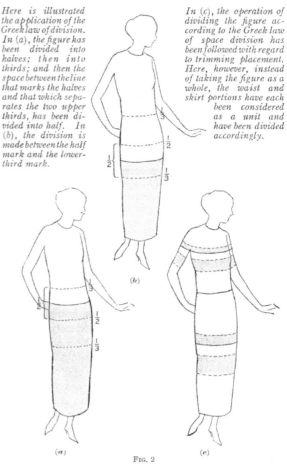

Here is illustrated the application of the Greek law of division. In (a), the figure has been divided into halves; then into thirds; and then the space between the line that marks the halves and that which separates the two upper thirds, has been divided into half. In (b), the division is made between the half mark and the lower-third mark.

In (c), the operation of dividing the figure according to the Greek law of space division has been followed with regard to trimming placement. Here, however, instead of taking the figure as a whole, the waist and skirt portions have each been considered as a unit and have been divided accordingly.

FIG. 2

THE GREEK LAW

TO dress in fashion is not enough. You must dress with sufficient becomingness and individuality to make it appear as though Fashion had shaped herself to your individual needs rather than that you had conceded to her. To achieve this effect, you must be familiar with proportions, balanced designs, depths and values of color, and, most essential of all, with the principles of design.

There are certain principles of design that can be applied to all types of women and costumes—the elements of proportion and scale, the principles of space division, the effect of light and dark spaces on the size of the figure, as well as the use of line to produce illusions of height or width. If these are well understood and applied, the result will be an expression of individual becomingness.

Principles of the Greek Law.—The Greek law of space division, which was applied to all the beautiful works of art created by the ancient Greeks, is of just as much importance at the present time as then. So, every one interested in the designing of clothes should understand this law and apply it. As shown in Fig. 1, the Greek law works on the theory that in dividing a

8

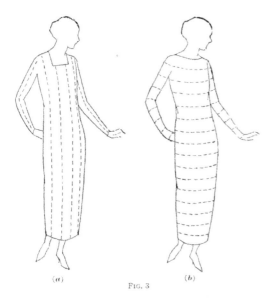

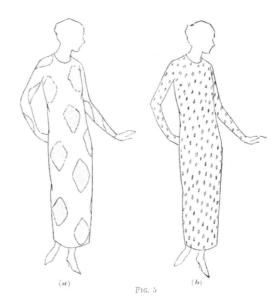

(a)　　　FIG. 3　　　(b)

(a)　　　FIG. 5　　　(b)

half the space between c and d and draw the heavy line f. You then have the two divisions af and fb. Now divide the lower part of the space, or fb, by means of the same principle. Dividing it in half, you get the division indicated by the dotted line g, and into thirds, you get the divisions indicated by h and i. Then divide the space between g and i, and you get the division marked by the heavy line j. This space is then divided into the two parts fj and jb, which is a less monotonous division than if divided into exact halves or thirds.

Note how the lines in the Grecian costume at the right in Fig. 1 bear out this principle of division.

In Fig. 2 are shown three examples of the crosswise division of space on the human figure. In (a) and (b), the distance from the base of the neck to the hem line has been divided into two unequal parts by the Greek law of division. Where contrasting blouse and

(a)　　　FIG. 4　　　(b)

skirt sections are desired, this form of division will prove a great aid in deciding the length of the blouse.

Such division of the space will prove a valuable aid in determining also the position of trimming, as shown in view (c), where the figure has been divided and subdivided into unequal spaces to secure a pleasing result.

CONTROLLING APPARENT SIZE OF FIGURE

Illusionary Effects Produced by Lines.—As shown in Fig. 3, certain lines give the impression of greater height and others give the effect of breadth. The figure in view (a), because of its many vertical lines, which carry the eye up and down, seems slenderer than that in (b), where horizontal lines create the effect of width. These two figures, however, are exactly the same size.

Curved lines can be employed to give length or to shorten an area. For instance, in Fig. 4, view (a), the downward curving lines at the neck and waist make the upper portion of the figure seem longer and more slender than it really is. The downward curve of the trimming line in the skirt also tends to emphasize the impression of height by carrying the eye still further down. In view (b), the wider angle of the neck line directed toward the upward curving waist line makes the upper portion of the figure become shorter in effect.

Effect of Light and Dark Areas.—Consider next the effect of light and dark surfaces on the figure. As illustrated in Fig. 5 (a), large patches of dark isolated in a large, white space, or large patches of light on dark, tend to increase the apparent size of the figure; whereas, a small, all-over design, as illustrated in (b), gives the impression of a flat area and does not alter the apparent size at all. If a pattern of large dimen-

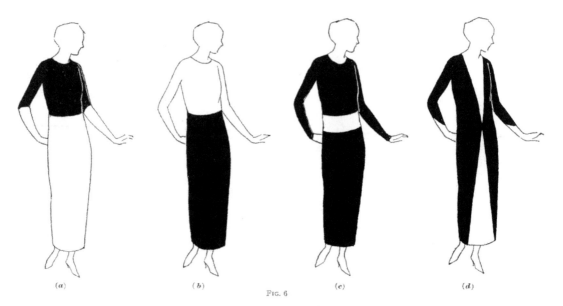

sions is to be used and it is too large to be becoming to the type of person who is to wear the dress, plait or drape the material so that the pattern is lost or blurred and the lines of the dress rather than the figures in the material, are most prominent. This applies to garments designed for both large and small persons.

It is well known that an entirely dark dress is less conspicuous than a light one and that it makes the figure seem smaller. Since this is true, it follows that if you wish to make any part of the body seem smaller than another, you should cover it with darker material; and, vice versa, if you wish to make any part of the body seem larger, you should cover it with a light color. In Fig. 6, views (a) and (b), this point is illustrated, the skirt section of (a) and the bodice section of (b) seeming larger and more prominent than their respective dark surfaces.

A light area in a garment that is dark in tone seems much larger by contrast; therefore, use great care in applying light decoration or ornament. In view (c), the light area at the waist line, contrasted with the darker areas which surround it, increase the apparent size of the waist. In view (d), the light sections seem to become the prominent parts of the figure and cause the eye to focus on the point where the two angles meet.

One of the most frequent errors in dress is the incorrect use of lines at the waist line. Some dress artists taboo entirely the blouse and skirt, insisting that the break in line caused by the difference in color and fabric spoils completely the unit of line of the human figure. But again and again Fashion brings forth the divided costume and one wishing to adapt it may successfully do so if the rule of correct proportion is followed and the individual size is always carefully considered.

In all your designing and planning, try to cultivate a feeling for scale, remembering that a small person must not be decorated with large details nor a large person with minute and dainty little trifles of trimming.

Remember, too, that a design must have unity; the parts must seem to belong together and the entire design look as though nothing could be added to, or taken from, it without detracting from the effect.

DESIGNING GARMENTS FOR YOURSELF

Securing Becoming Proportions and Pleasing
Style Effects Through Individual Designing

METHOD OF PLANNING CLOTHES

PATTERN designers and manufacturers are of the opinion that women select their designs and patterns before they purchase their materials and trimmings. Yet every woman knows what it is to be lured by a beautiful piece of material in the shops and to purchase it without having in mind a definite design or definite plans for making. Practically every woman has been guilty, at one time or another, of buying a beautiful piece of trimming, hoping to find a design and fabric that would go with it perfectly. But much the safer plan, before buying material, is to be well informed as to the silhouette, the style tendency, and the fabrics favored, and to decide tentatively what phase of the new mode you are going to try to express.

After studying the fashions and deciding tentatively on the color, the fabric, and the trimming, consider whether your choice will necessitate new accessories, such as hat, wrap, shoes, or gloves. Sometimes, when such is the case, you can compromise on color or material and fit the dress into your wardrobe at a minimum of expense.

Learning the Season's Tendencies.—Material and color having been decided on, you are ready to consider the matter of a design that is suitable for you and in keeping with the silhouette. In the main, the manner of making and finishing garments is not so important as the silhouette, which means the general contour, the length and fulness of the skirt, the shape of the sleeve and of the collar, as well as the position of the waist line and its tendency toward snugness or looseness.

If you make a dress slightly short-waisted and the tendency for a longer waist is coming to the fore, the dress will, no doubt, appear passé before its time.

Any winter dress should be designed so as to be safe for wear for two seasons, or for three, with changes of trimming. A summer dress should be planned to be good for two seasons. A dress that is smart only for the moment is an extravagance that few can afford.

Learn, therefore, through study and observation, which way the pendulum of fashion will swing and then swing with it. Observe fashion drawings rather than advertisements picturing ready-to-wear clothing, because the manufacturer determines his designs six to eight months in advance, while the style magazine is prepared only about three months in advance.

Subscribe to a good, reliable, fashion magazine—one that shows style tendencies. There are several women's magazines that have very satisfactory fashion and pattern departments. The competition existing between them makes them eager to present their very best to the advantage of the woman subscriber. Besides subscribing to one of these magazines—the one whose patterns you prefer—take, if possible, a magazine noted for its style value. In addition to these, when ultra-smart frocks are desired, the occasional buying of a French magazine is advantageous.

GIVING REALITY TO YOUR IDEAS

After studying fashion magazines until you are familiar with the season's tendencies, you are in a position to apply the ideas thus gained in designing for yourself. You may plan your gowns so that they embody becoming style features, and do it correctly, if you but learn to trace fashion designs and then to divide the outline into becomingly correct proportions.

Try for yourself. You may not be satisfied with your first or even your tenth attempt, but by trying, by thinking out designs with the aid of pencil and tissue paper, you will eventually be able to decide quite definitely all points concerning a dress design. And then you can undertake its making with the assurance of a right and satisfying effect.

Method of Designing.—For practice and to develop the idea, select from among the outlines of the human figure, shown on the pages that follow, the one whose silhouette as nearly as possible represents your type. Then, placing a piece of transparent paper over it, trace lightly the outline of the neck, shoulders, and upper arms; also, trace very lightly the side lines and the dotted lines, indicating the center front of the figure and the normal waist line.

Next, using this outline as a foundation, mark around it the silhouette of the type of garment you wish. Then put in clearly the principal lines of your design—the construction lines and the lines that represent trimming. It should be understood that the construction lines of a garment correspond with the actual pattern lines, whereas the trimming lines are purely decorative and may be placed wherever they are most effective.

A knowledge of pattern cutting and draping will serve you well here, for it will help you to avoid lines that cut up the garment too much or that cannot be translated into corresponding lines in the cutting and hanging of the material. All lines must, of course, conform with the principles of design and suitability previously given.

As you do this work, consider all points carefully—the neck line, the sleeve length, the waist and hem lines, the opening of the dress, the laundering, etc. Decide on the color, material, and trimming, and determine your reason for making each selection.

This is as near as you can come to class-room training, working alone, but such practice will help you concentrate on a dress design in its entirety and develop your sense of proportion, scale, and line. It is not necessary for you to know much about draw-

(a)   Fig. 8   (b)

ing in order to do such work. Use your own ideas; make a memorandum of any part not clear to you; then, as you study, work to find the solution.

In considering a design, take it apart during your calculation in order to see what its base, or foundation, lines are and what there is new about it. This not only helps in selecting a substantial fashion, but aids greatly in achieving just the right style effect.

TYPES OF FIGURES
THE IDEAL FIGURE

The individual so fortunate as to possess the ideal figure, which is illustrated in Fig. 7, may feel that she can wear anything and look well. While this is true to a certain extent, on her, as on any one else, falls the responsibility of avoiding the commonplace and of choosing right colors as well as garments that suit her type, her age, and the purpose and occasion for which the garment is desired.

Designing for the Ideal Figure.—The ideal type, fortunate in being able to wear lines that cut across as well as those that run up and down the figure, is the easiest of all types for which to design garments. Fig. 8, view (a), illustrates the first step in designing a gown for this type. To prepare a sketch similar to this, trace the outlines of the neck, the shoulders, the arms, and the side lines of Fig. 7, as well as the dotted lines indicating the center front and the normal waist line; and build the silhouette, or skeleton lines, of the garment upon this foundation.

After the general shape, or outline, is secured, the

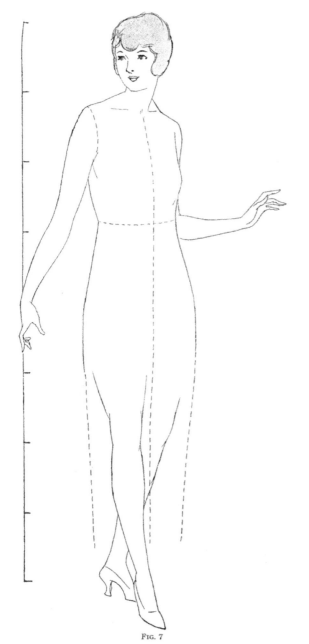

Fig. 7

(a)   Fig. 9   (b)

You will observe that not only the lines, but the light and dark sections of the gown in Fig. 8, cut the figure crosswise, a permissible division for the ideal type, as she has no cause to fear increasing the apparent breadth of any portion of her figure.

The gown in Fig. 9 also is planned for the ideal type. View (a) shows the position and direction of the construction and trimming lines. The crosswise lines that so pleasingly break the length of the silhouette have been reproduced in view (b) by means of the small tier on the skirt; the lines running parallel with the dotted center-front line as far as the skirt tier have given place to the tasseled, ribbon band; while the slanting lines in the upper part of the waist have been brought out by the collar arrangement. Instead of the ribbon and the lace collar, embroidery or braiding might have been used, this following the trimming lines shown in view (a).

Applying Designing Instruction to Other Figures. In this way, the designs of the various garments that follow have been developed. View (a) gives, in each instance, the skeleton lines of the gown in view (b). As you study these models, keep this relationship of view (a) to view (b) in mind, following out in your imagination each step in the process of working out the various designs. The value of such practice can hardly be overestimated, for the familiarity with correct working methods which it gives you, will help you greatly in designing and planning clothes that will be a credit to you.

You will observe that the ideal type is just 8 heads high from the top of the head to the base of the foot on which the weight is thrown. The scale at the side of each figure will enable you to see how it differs from the ideal in height. All the figures have the silhouette of the well-corseted and properly brassièred human form, and the designs can be planned over them as over the figure of the woman herself.

position and general direction of the construction and trimming lines are determined. Because of the simplicity of the design at this stage, it is a comparatively easy matter to obtain a pleasing relationship of these lines. But this is, nevertheless, a most important step in the development of a garment, for upon the pleasing relationship of its construction and trimming lines depends much of its success or failure.

As you work, therefore, experiment with lines and spaces until you are sure that you have secured the most pleasing result possible. Watch each experiment closely, observing the effect of crosswise and up-and-down lines, short lines, and long lines that run from the waist into the skirt, thus drawing the whole dress into a unit instead of dividing it into a waist and a skirt section. By means of such practice, your eye will become trained and sensitive to the slightest variations of proportions.

View (b) shows how the lines indicated in (a) are developed into an attractive model. The slightly diagonal lines at the center front of the skirt in view (a) were used to produce an inverted box plait; the tapering lines at the neck were developed into a convertible collar; the lowest of the three parallel crosswise lines became the waist line; the line above became the line of the joining of the waist and skirt sections; and the uppermost line became a trimming line. The idea of the little V-shaped dip in this trimming line with its wee bit of embroidery came afterward. General lines and directions must always be decided on first; then, as you work out your design, the little details will take care of themselves.

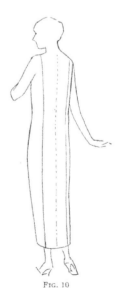

In working out a design for the back of a garment, trace this silhouette and use it as a foundation, modifying it as may be necessary to secure the outline you desire. Follow the process already described of first tracing the silhouette and then putting in the principal lines of your design—the construction lines and the lines that represent trimming.

As the figure is turned a little toward the side, giving a three-quarter rather than a straight back view, the position of the center-back line is just a little to the right of the exact center. The lines on each side are guide lines that will help you in case you may wish to use a panel arrangement or vertical lines of trimming.

Fig. 10

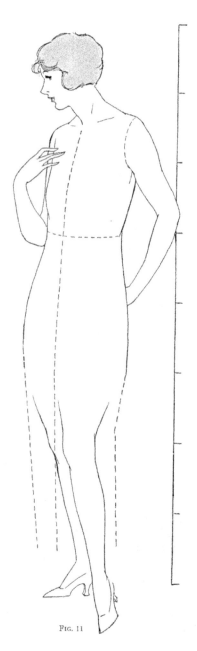

FIG. 11

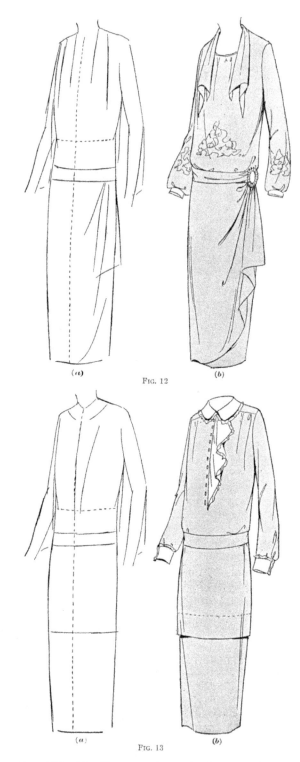

FIG. 12

FIG. 13

SLIGHTLY DROOPING FIGURE

The slightly drooping figure, Fig. 11, often that of the mature woman, must work for easy grace and for a softening of all lines that tend toward severity. She should, of course, avoid severely tailored costumes, choosing instead flowing lines and gracefully draped effects, as illustrated by the draped collar and the side drape of the skirt in Fig. 12. The graceful long sleeve and the soft, not too revealing, neck line are also features of becomingness.

Plaited or gathered frills, as in Fig. 13, are suited to her type, as are also blouse fronts that are full but not too cut up in design. If the drooping figure inclines toward the tall, slender type, the crosswise line in the skirt of Fig. 13 will prove a becoming feature. Desirable, also, for her in concealing hollows and angles are the Buster Brown collar and the long sleeves.

In general, the woman with a drooping, mature figure may indulge in anything that emphasizes dignity and charm or is fluffy without being frivolous.

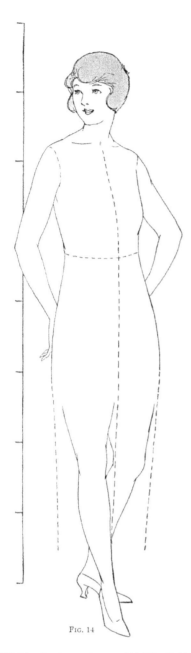

FIG. 14

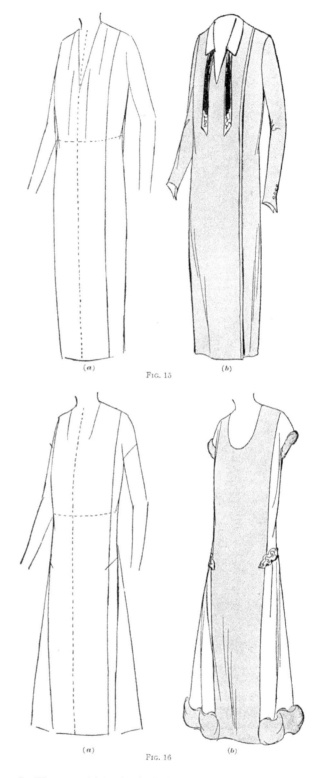

(a)   FIG. 15   (b)

(a)   FIG. 16   (b)

SHORT, WELL-PROPORTIONED FIGURE

The short, well-proportioned figure, shown in Fig. 14, should not find the planning of clothes difficult. The lines of her garments should always be long; the surface design, simple and not cut up into numerous small areas. The flaring skirt, the long drape from shoulder to hem, the V- or U-neck line, are all desirable features for her. All trimming applied to her costumes should be in proportion to her stature, small and dainty.

The tailored simplicity of the gown in Fig. 15, the absence of a defined waist line, the V-shaped neck line, the small, trim collar, the long tie ends, and the long tight sleeves, all contribute to the effect of height.

In Fig. 16, which also is designed for the short, well-proportioned woman, the most noticeable feature is the full-length panel. To prevent the waist line from interfering with the long line of the panel, it is merely indicated at the side.

15

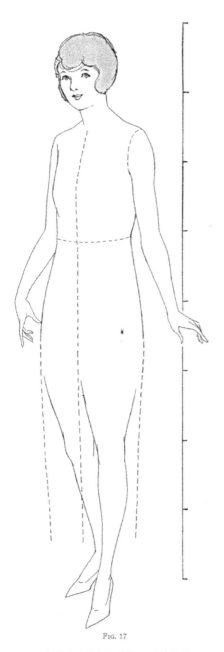

FIG. 17

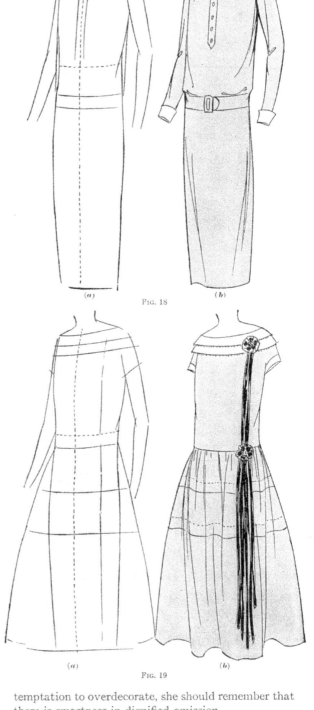

FIG. 18

FIG. 19

BOYISH, IMMATURE FIGURE

Youthfulness and simplicity should be the keynote of dress designs for the boyish, immature figure, illustrated in Fig. 17. Tailored effects, as in Fig. 18, are suited to her type, evidencing the simplest lines with the most moderate trimming, such as the Buster Brown collar, the small neat cuffs, the leather belt, and the diminutive tie.

For her, also, are afternoon or evening dresses that spell youth—dresses with plaits, flounces, flaring skirts, round neck lines, short sleeves, high waist lines or no waist lines at all. She must not, however, indulge in ornate ornamentation, elaborate drapes, or exotic or sophisticated effects. Whenever she feels the temptation to overdecorate, she should remember that there is smartness in dignified omission.

Basques with billowy skirts, one of which is in Fig. 19, are charming for this type. Youthful also are the collar arrangement and the abbreviated sleeves. The trimming shown gives a touch of distinctiveness.

FIG. 20

FIG. 21

(a)   (b)

(a)   FIG. 22   (b)

TALL, STATELY FIGURE

The tall, stately figure, shown in Fig. 20, reminds one of the Greek statues, and like them, this type can wear clinging, flowing drapes with distinction. Her sleeves and skirts must not be too short, and she must shun all ruffles, flares, or features that suggest fussiness. In fact, for her, also, smartness lies largely in simplicity—in what is left off rather than in what is put on. Her costumes should be rich and regal, all decoration being to scale; that is, not too small. The contour of her face should determine the neck line.

Note the pleasing arrangement of the lines of embroidery and the tunic in Fig. 21. The waist line is placed considerably below the normal waist.

In the evening dress, shown in Fig. 22, the long, graceful lines of the drape are most desirable, and the tunic effect modifies the height of the figure.

17

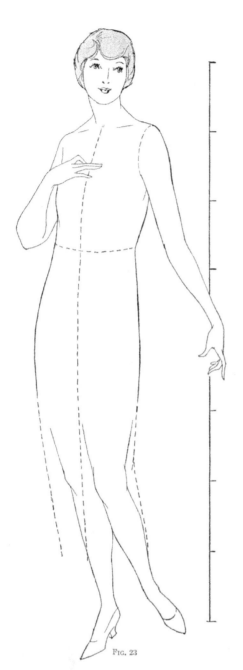

FIG. 23

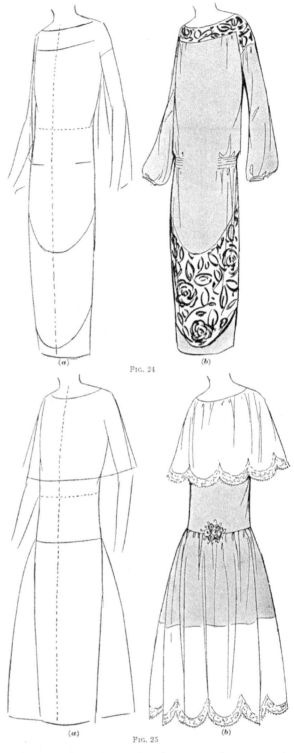

FIG. 24

FIG. 25

TALL, SLENDER FIGURE

As the tall, slender type, shown in Fig. 23, is often too thin, she has many points to consider. To modify her height, crosswise effects, not only lines but areas of light and dark that run across, should be employed in designing her costumes. Also, decoration and ornament should be used in crosswise effect, as in Fig. 24, instead of up and down. The type of sleeve in this gown, a sleeve that is long but not close-fitting, is most becoming to the tall, slender woman. For evening, she may wear sleeves that are flowing.

Fig. 25 shows an evening gown designed for her. Note the areas of light and dark running crosswise and the wide collar which increases the apparent breadth of the figure and covers the angles of the shoulders and the thinness of the upper arms.

Short skirts are becoming to women of this type, either skirts of the extended variety, as in Fig. 25, or skirts with tiers or plaited flounces.

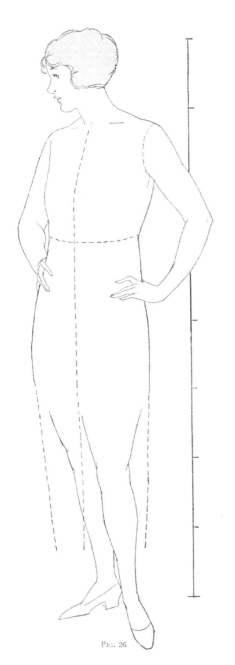

FIG. 26

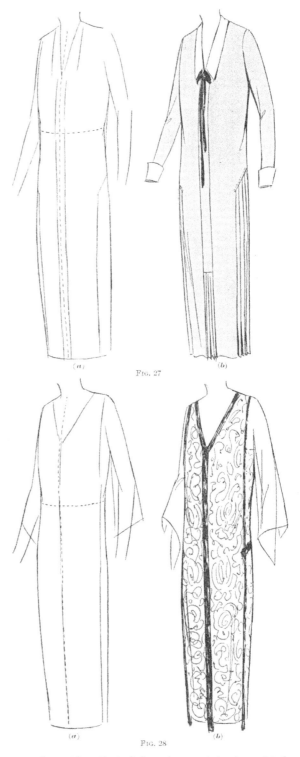

(a)   FIG. 27   (b)

(a)   FIG. 28   (b)

ATHLETIC FIGURE

The athletic, broad-shouldered type, shown in Fig. 26, must avoid tight-fitting bodices, full skirts, and very short sleeves. She has many of the attributes of the tall, stately figure and can, to a certain extent, wear clothes that are similar. But she will be most suitably dressed in a strictly tailored costume, though she must be careful to overcome any appearance of angularity.

The dress in Fig. 27 is especially suited to her—the close-fitting sleeves, the plain collar and cuffs, the string tie, the whole effect of tailored simplicity.

Because of her broad shoulders, her sleeve line or any decoration that defines it, must be brought in toward the neck line, and the top of the sleeve must be very smooth. An excellent arrangement is suggested in Fig. 28, where the dark beaded band, running the entire length of the garment on each side, conveys the idea of slenderness and cuts the width of the shoulders.

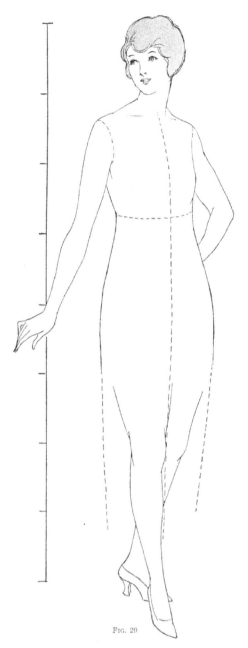

FIG. 29

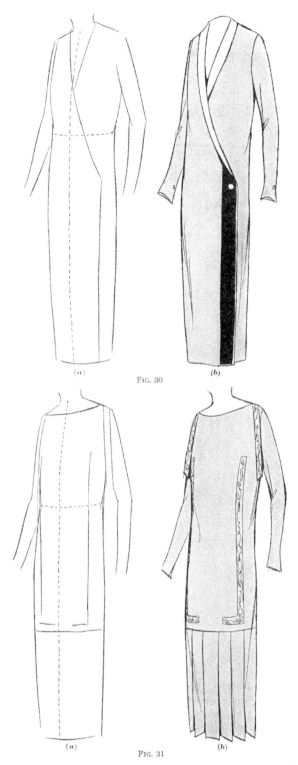

(a) FIG. 30 (b)

(a) FIG. 31 (b)

SHORT-WAISTED FIGURE

The woman who, as shown in Fig. 29, is short-waisted, whose hips are a little larger than normal, and whose shoulders and bust are a little narrower, though she is of average dimensions in every other respect, should design her costumes so that lines fall from the outermost point of her shoulders to a point well below the hips. Her waist line should be placed quite low and never sharply defined. Her neck lines and collar lines should be broad and there should be definite up-and-down lines in the skirt portion of the garment.

In Fig. 30, the eye follows the line of the collar to a point below the waist line and on to the bottom of the skirt, the wide dark band of trimming on the skirt diminishing the apparent width of the hips.

In Fig. 31, the very low cross-line in the skirt gives the effect of an extremely low waist line. The trimming of the upper portion of the waist gives width to the shoulders, thus balancing the width of the hips.

FIG. 32

FIG. 33

FIG. 34

LARGE, ROUND FIGURE

Fig. 32 shows the large, round figure.   Like her tall, stately sister, the woman with this type of figure may wear clinging, graceful, up-and-down drapes, but the smooth-fitting, straight-hanging costume will prove most satisfactory.   Such a costume is shown in Fig. 33, the large surfaces of which have been broken up with vertical lines.   The long, tight sleeves are a becoming feature, as are also the small collar, the V neck, and the vestee with its vertical line of buttons.

Fig. 34 illustrates another straight-line frock designed for the large, round type.   Here again are the long, tight sleeves and surfaces broken up by vertical lines, a note of interest, however, being provided by the oblique, or slanting, line of the skirt. The collar arrangement and the shape of the neck line show variety, a square neck line being permissible when the dress does not seem to call for a V neck.

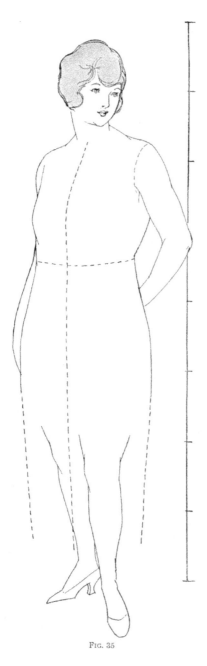

FIG. 35

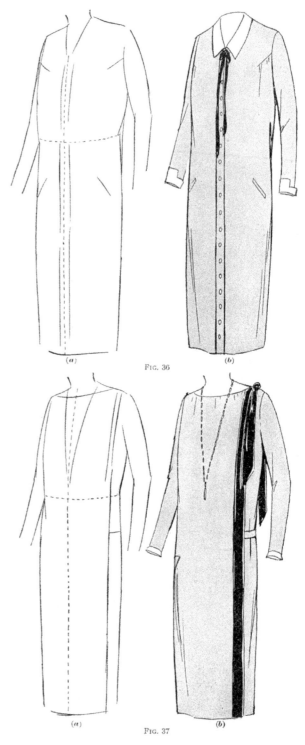

FIG. 36

FIG. 37

SHORT, ROUND FIGURE

The suggestions given for the large, round figure are applicable to the short, round figure, shown in Fig. 35, except that *all* crosswise lines must be avoided. Lines that are absolutely vertical or that may be divided into vertical areas of light and dark, or long lines in the form of groups of plaits or tucks or other lengthwise trimming may be utilized.

In Fig. 36, the tie ends and buttons conspire to produce an illusion of height; in Fig. 37, the tie and the band trimming contribute to this effect. The long, plain sleeves are, of course, suitable for this type, as is also the V-neck line of the dress in Fig. 36. If the face is not too round, the type of neck line in Fig. 37 is also quite suitable and makes the distance from the neck to the hem line seam as long as possible. A pleasing way of making the bateau neck line less obvious and of giving an up-and-down line, is the addition of a string of beads, as suggested in the illustration.

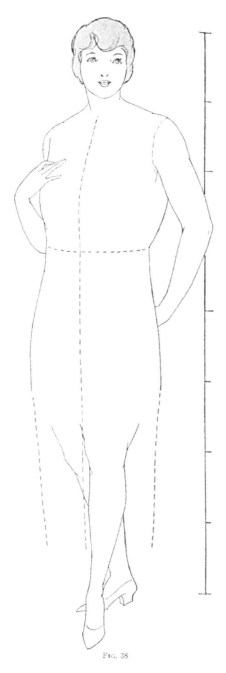

FIG. 38

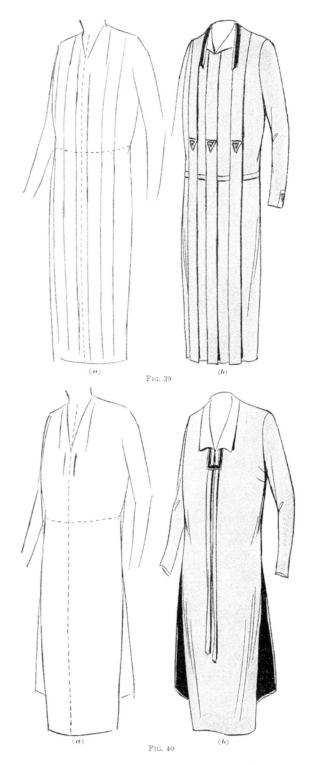

FIG. 39

FIG. 40

FIGURE LARGE ABOVE THE WAIST

For the figure large above the waist, shown in Fig. 38, vertical lines are in order. But, in designing the bodice of a garment for this type, do not have a large light area, such as a vest in a dark dress, extend to the waist line or lower, for this will only tend to emphasize the curves of the bust.

Long lines can be achieved by box plaits, as in Fig. 39. Here the position of the unobtrusive decoration above the normal waist line lengthens the effect of the lower part of the figure and shortens that of the upper part, thus distributing the proportions.

In Fig. 40, the godets add width to the skirt, thereby tending to balance the upper portion of the body, but they must not flare very much beyond the outline of the figure. The novel arrangement of the tie with its long ends adds interest and provides a slenderizing line to this rather plain model.

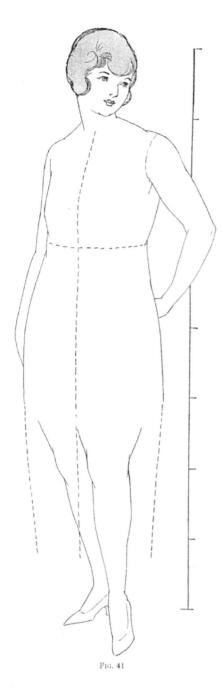

FIG. 41

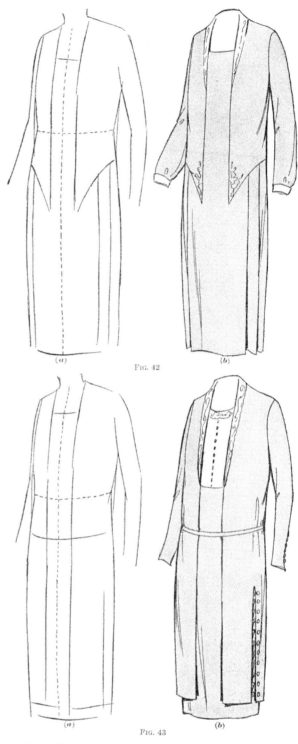

FIG. 42

FIG. 43

FIGURE LARGE BELOW THE WAIST

A difficult task lies before the woman who, as in Fig. 41, is large below the waist; but it is not impossible for her to achieve the beautiful. She must place her waist line very low, never drawing in her dress at the normal waist line. In the back, the dress must fall straight from the shoulders to the hips, while the skirt should be divided into numerous vertical sections. She may wear surplice effects if her bust is small.

In Fig. 42, the long-waisted effect has been achieved by the two downward curving lines of the waist, these being emphasized by the vertical lines that meet them and by the embroidery. The lines of the plaits tend to diminish the apparent width of the hips.

She may wear the light vest effect illustrated in Fig. 43, provided there are lines that carry the eye down. The width of the skirt here is judiciously cut into sections and the line of the tunic aids in balancing the proportions of waist and skirt sections.

DESIGNING FOR THE STOUT FIGURE

Creating an Illusion of Slenderness by the Application of Certain Well-Defined Principles

CONCEALING EXTRA POUNDS

APPLYING SLENDERIZING PRINCIPLES

DESIGNERS throughout the country say that the biggest problem of the ready-to-wear manufacturer is to develop dresses that are becoming to women who are overweight. One finds in the ready-to-wear shops so-called "slenderizing stouts" to be sure, but many times such models merely call attention to stoutness. Besides, they are generally for matronly women, rather than for those who wish to look young and smart. It seems practically impossible to get youthful and appropriate clothes for women who wear sizes over 38. Yet it may be necessary only to change a neck line, remove an ornament, or alter the line of a sleeve in order to transform a "dumpy fat woman's dress" into a model of slender grace and youthful charm.

The whole art of appearing slender rests on certain scientific principles. Learn these and you can know beforehand that *every* dress, *every* coat, *every* garment you wear will be designed to give you height instead of width, youth instead of matronliness, slenderness and grace instead of heaviness. In fact, through the application of these principles, you can always know just what to select to make your particular type of figure look as slim and well-proportioned as you wish.

As you look through fashion books, don't discredit all the styles, saying they are planned only for the slim. Study them carefully, find a collar from one, a waist line from another, and fabric suggestions from still another. Remember that you have a great many good points and try to bring them out. Dress to be fashionable, but learn to discriminate so that you can find the best for you in the new and can conceal intelligently and comfortably your few extra pounds.

DISCRIMINATE USE OF DETAILS

Remember continually, too, that it isn't the dress alone that you need to watch, but every slight detail, for the little things can destroy the big. For instance, eyeglasses can accentuate a round face or slenderize it, depending upon their prominence and shape. Buttons can stick out and look bulky; blouses, when worn with different color skirts, can cut you in two; and belts of different color from that of skirt or blouse can prove even more treacherous. Gloves or shoes that are too small give your size away. Lacy stockings emphasize where they shouldn't and are as faulty as they are expensive.

Buy a few things and have everything right.

Think of all of your wardrobe at one time. Be sure that everything goes together agreeably. Take care to keep every part of your clothing in good repair and immaculately clean. Every woman can gain a reputation for being well-dressed if she remembers not to be haphazard in buying, wearing, and caring for her clothes.

Avoid every tendency toward overdress. Don't trim yourself too much. Modest simplicity—intricate simplicity, perhaps, but a beautiful simplicity—is a definite part of the stout woman's program and must be followed out religiously to conceal at all times an extra 30 or 40 pounds.

CORRECT FOUNDATIONS

Corsets.—Although this is termed the corsetless age, the best-dressed women are still wearing corsets and will continue to wear them because they realize the necessity of retaining lovely curves and lines. And when the slender woman is careful about her corset, what must the responsibility of the large woman be? It is just this: she must wear a good corset and she must select it with such care and have it fitted with such perfection that even she can forget it once she has put it on. No evidence of a corset is ever seen on a correctly dressed woman.

Don't ever let your modesty or your pride keep you from being fitted properly. All merchants and corsetières expect to fit the corsets they sell. They know their stock better than you do and realize that a proper corset can definitely and permanently help in correct-

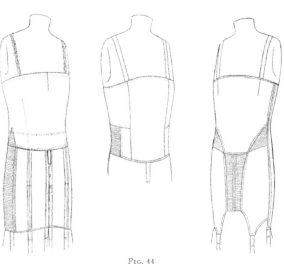

FIG. 44

ing line, molding it easily and gracefully, and making a satisfied customer for them. A full-proportioned figure is ugly only when it runs over. Graceful, even curves are pleasing to see, and large figures can make their own curves graceful if they will.

Always sit down in your corset, when it is being fitted, to make sure that the stays in the front are not too long. If necessary, have them shortened, as this may be easily done and will produce a much better-fitting corset. You cannot comfortably sit reared back as is necessary when the stays are too long.

Brassières.—Brassières are as necessary as corsets. They should never be so tight as to bind, but always close enough to give a smooth outer line, high enough to confine the bust perfectly, and long enough to come down well over the corset so that an unbroken waist line is attained. Fig. 44 shows three good foundations for the stout figure.

Other Undergarments.—Knitted underwear is usually desirable for stout figures as it clings more closely than do the woven varieties. But you needn't confine yourself to the ordinary kind, because with a little ingenuity, you can trim a plain, inexpensive, ready-made piece attractively with bands or strips of lace, straight-line fashion, and give it a dainty, hand-

made look. Undergarments, similar to those illustrated in Fig. 45, are suggested for slenderness.

Omit unnecessary fulness at the top of lingerie, using tiny lengthwise darts to fit the garments close and smooth. Avoid ruffles, all gathers at the waist line, and bulk at any place, fitting the garment so smoothly that not a wrinkle or line is visible when the dress is on.

After following these really simple rules in regard to underthings, you are ready to give your attention to the dress, wrap, and hat, but don't underestimate the necessity for smooth, perfectly-fitting underwear, corset, brassière, and slip, for without attention to these details, you cannot possibly acquire the correctly slender appearance that you desire.

LINES THAT SLENDERIZE

To create an impression of slenderness, the dominate lines in a design must be vertical, never horizontal. The light and dark areas must run up and down, never across, and these must be used with discretion or the figure will seem divided into many parts, thus giving greater width. Skirts must not be too short, the waist line must not be confined or emphasized, and curved effects must be avoided.

There are many ways in which the effect of a costume can be ruined. For instance, if a band of fur is added to the bottom of the skirt of a perfectly straight line dress of correct lines, the up-and-down line will be broken at the bottom and the appearance of the figure shortened and widened considerably.

Another point to be very careful about is the matter of straight lines. The tall, slender effect you hoped to gain by the lengthwise lines of your costume may be entirely ruined if you apply trimmings of any kind which radiate outwards toward these lines. A woman dressed in a gown that has uninterrupted, harmonious lines looks taller, slenderer, more dignified, and in every way more pleasing than a woman, the radiating lines of whose gown make her figure seem to bulge outwards.

Fig. 46 illustrates the value of emphasizing a long line by the trick of placing it between two longer ones. Shorter bands of trimming, placed on each side of the center band, would have the effect of *shortening* its appearance. By the application of this seemingly unimportant trifle, the figure is made to seem slenderer, taller, and smarter.

Fig. 47 shows how a long, slim effect may be created by parallel lines which emphasize an oblique, or slanting, line. A plain, unbroken, oblique line draws attention to its width. Without the two parallel bands of trimming, the oblique hem line of the tunic skirt would, therefore, *appear* wider and more horizontal than it does in the illustration. But the parallel lines, that break it emphasize the effect of length and make it seem more graceful.

It is such tricks as these which our eyes play on us and which must be taken into account by women who

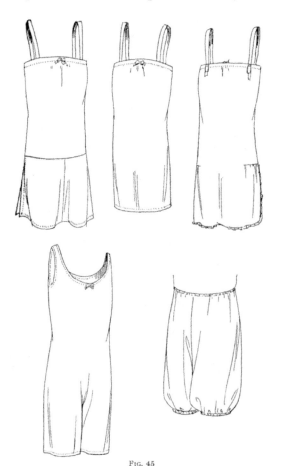

FIG. 45

FIG. 46　　　　　FIG. 47

wish to look slender. Not only very stout, but moderately stout and even slender women should bear these principles in mind, for even the slender woman can lose all the advantage of her slim silhouette and actually appear stout by failing to dress in accordance with these laws. A badly designed gown or wrap may easily give her the appearance of being many pounds heavier than she really is, and it is appearance that counts. *You* may know what the scales say, but other people will weigh you with the eye.

SLENDERIZING NECK LINES

In order to counteract the roundness and provide some contrast for the fulness of the face, it is usually best to decide on a neck line emphasizing angles, not curves. Always have the dress cut well up at the back but let it drop down with straight lines to a deep V or square in front. It is wise to have the neck line cut low and to fill in the opening with sheer Georgette, batiste, or lace in an inconspicuous color, such as delicate flesh or deep cream.

The short, stout figure with a short neck and medium small head is one type of stout that can wear a U-neck line or a slightly rounding neck line becomingly, for such a neck line makes the head and neck appear larger and gives a good balance.

A necklace that is slender, well-made, and plain, such as illustrated in Fig. 48, is a real asset to a stout woman, as it helps the collar line, slenderizes the face, and gives an appearance of length over the front that is pleasing. But by all means avoid heavy crystals,

and don't ever wear beads unless they give a definitely desirable lengthening effect.

SLEEVES FOR LARGE ARMS

If your arms are fat, don't wear long-shouldered dresses or kimono sleeves for they just aren't meant for you. From the points of style, becomingness, and service, they will fail you all the way. On the other hand, don't overdo narrow shoulders. Rather, work for a happy medium.

Upper arms that are larger than the armhole are quite common, and the mistake is often made of fitting the armhole to the sleeve rather than the sleeve to the armhole. Have the armhole comfortable and, if necessary, set a gusset in the sleeves or increase the seams in cutting from the armhole to the elbow.

A woman, who was wearing size 44 dresses that hung on her unattractively and heavily, said that she couldn't get her arms into the sleeves of size 40 or 42 models. A wise saleswoman ripped the sleeve seams, inserted gussets, and molded her beautifully into a tailored frock, size 40. Since then she looks 20 pounds lighter, all because of this little adjustment.

A bias sleeve is sometimes a distinct advantage for a stout arm. Take flannel or the heavy crêpes. A "tight as the skin" sleeve may be fitted which has "give" enough for comfort, yet not a quarter of an inch surplus. This type of sleeve is not suitable for flimsy materials, but is very good for the firmer fabrics and is sometimes economical for cutting, as often the sleeve pattern can be placed on a true bias grain to advantage.

One clever designer makes for her larger customers a firm-net foundation waist with close-fitting sleeves extending almost to the elbow. This protects the dress and has the advantage of confining the arms slightly.

There are many details in sleeves to consider when you wish to appear smaller than you actually are. Your success will be due largely to your knowledge and its right application. So watch, look, and listen for every hint that will aid you in expressing perfection. Every achievement stimulates greater desire and effort.

Here are illustrated three slender, well-made necklaces, the unique and attractive character of which would make them a desirable addition to a plain gown. Their length and slenderness suit them particularly to the stout figure when a lengthening line is desired.

FIG. 48

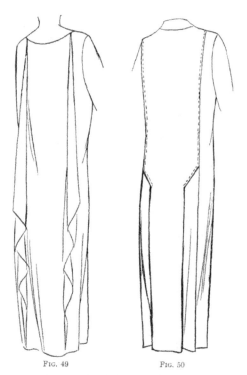

FIG. 49   FIG. 50

COLLARS FOR FLESHY SHOULDERS

Large shoulders are a problem because they can appear quite as full as the bust and by their roundness add years, which, of course, nobody wants. A collar that is just right in depth, not too deep nor too short in the back, is the first essential. For your individual type, you must make experiments. Take a piece of muslin or paper and cut out modish collars that you think would be becoming to you. Then with the aid of two mirrors, try them on and view the back, front, and sides, examining well down past the waist line because the collar line and belt line must always agree. Turn under the collar edge or add to it, or, after careful observation, do whatever else your eye tells you is best.

Never let your collar be so long as to look like a cape unless it is a cape; and don't let it be of a length or size to lie up on your back like a doily on a table. Attach it—have it there for a purpose, that of giving a correct and becoming line.

If you are full in the back, don't wear shoulder capes or bertha collars. Never wear heavy collars or babyish lace or ribbon, and avoid collars of vivid color that contrast definitely with the color of your dress.

SLEEVES THAT DISGUISE WEIGHT BELOW WAIST LINE

Of much importance for a figure with most of the weight below the waist are the design and the trimming of the sleeves. To plan for what should be gracefully flowing sleeves but usually turn out to be a tragedy of adding pounds to pounds, is a weakness

in which a stout woman must never indulge. In summer time and for evening wear, the sleeve may fit easily but without flare and may reach to a point just above the elbow, provided there is no trimming feature or cuff. For all other types of dresses, the long, close-fitting sleeve is wisest. By adding to, or taking from, the length of sleeves, emphasis may be given to any part of the body from the hip line up, as the bottom of a sleeve is naturally a line that will attract the eye. If this is in the wrong position, it is easy to imagine the result. Experiment with this feature, and convince yourself of the truth of the statement.

FULL BUSTS AND BROAD BACKS

When the bust is full and the skirt length is short, it is wise to use a panel effect in the front and let the belt or waist-line finish extend from side to side across the back, thus leaving an unbroken front line. As a rule, the large figure looks best in a very long waist line, but such a waist line is not desirable when the proportions are such that the upper part of the figure overbalances the lower part.

It is always wise for this type to beware of surplice-front dresses. The mature figure, flat in front, can wear a surplice very well and often it serves to relieve an undesirable plainness. Many fashion artists, when they draw full-bust figures, take special pains to put in surplice fronts, but experience shows that it is very difficult to duplicate in fabric the easy, smooth curve of the surplice indicated by the pencil.

And as surplice fronts are difficult for a very full

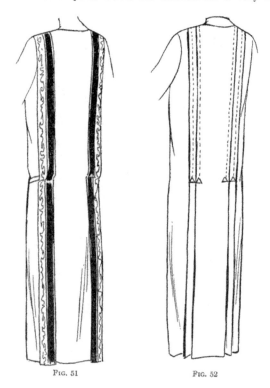

FIG. 51   FIG. 52

bust, so are plain backs on fat shoulders. If your back is full and round, remember to use tucks, bands, folds, plaits, or something that will definitely break the width. Panels also help, so don't be afraid to use them. Broad backs broken in width are far more pleasing than broad expanses that know no termination. Remember the panel can befriend you, so keep it close but use it only when it can compliment you. Figs. 49 to 54, inclusive, show six simple ways of decreasing the apparent width of the back.

SLENDERIZING TRIMMINGS

Think long and carefully about trimmings before choosing them because a misuse of decoration can mar the lines of an otherwise becoming gown.

Trimming, judiciously placed, will produce an appearance of smartness and, by its position, may break a wide, plain surface into two or perhaps three spaces, each line adding a point to the illusion of slenderness. Apply trimming to draw attention to a closing, to finish the edge of a panel, or for some other useful purpose.

Never use a large-figured trimming or a bright-colored banding. Plaids, big polka dots, pronounced stripes, heavily embroidered fabrics, or "gew gaws" are not for the big woman. Strive for distinctive lines which are, in themselves, simple. Wear as good-quality fabric as your purse can buy, but be modest about any decoration you employ.

Don't ever be tempted to wear frills, ruffles, tassels, or ornaments that wave about as you walk, for they double your size every time.

FIG. 55

Self-fabric, that is, the material of which the dress is made, is always good as trimming. It may be tucked or plaited and inserted between cut edges, applied as a band, or used to form a cord, which in turn forms ornaments of various shapes and sizes.

Small-patterned laces in the wider widths are appropriate, too, and add richness and dignity to clothes intended for dressy occasions. Lace should never be shirred for the stout woman, for, as already suggested, she can never afford to be frivolous in her dress, and ruffled lace would certainly make her so.

Plaited panels are good, but these should always be held close to the dress by the use of a French tack from 2 to 3 inches long. The groups of vertical lines formed by the plaits increase height effectively.

Ribbon banding is effective, both when stretched flat and when used to form long sash ends.

A WISE CHOICE OF WRAPS

First, beware of fur coats. Even though rich and luxurious, they are bulky and heavy in appearance.

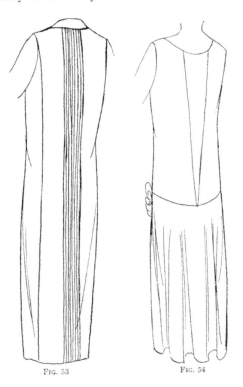

FIG. 53   FIG. 54

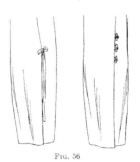

FIG. 56

As shown here, fasteners for coats should be placed at the side and be as inconspicuous as possible.

Trim, tailored coats with long simple lines, such as those illustrated in Fig. 55, are more flattering and less expensive, so think twice before you buy a fur coat. Buy lovely soft fabrics that are rich in quality and soft enough to "cling"—a word to remember and think about when you buy or plan a garment of any sort. Let your coat be unbroken in line and untrimmed. A large button set on the stomach can destroy more art than you can plan out in a month. As shown in Fig. 56, oblong buttons at the side or string ties of the material of the coat are best.

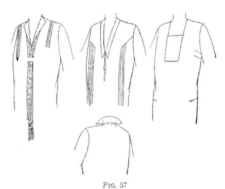

Fig. 57

Have your coat long or hip length. Watch the line carefully. There is a point that is becoming in length; make sure you find it.

If you are square-shouldered, you may find capes very becoming, but generally they add size rather than reduce it.

Long fur or fabric scarfs are desirable. Ostrich or ruffly scarfs, of course, are to be looked at with admiration for their softness and color, but rarely worn by anyone desiring a slenderizing effect.

CORRECT SHOES AND STOCKINGS

What kind of shoes and stockings do you wear? Surely, not pumps, for your weight is too great to be comfortable in them, and besides pumps will not give you the harmonious effect that you want to achieve in your costume. A bulge is sure to show at the top, which not only is uncomfortable for you but shows in itself that you are fat. Wear a strap or laced slipper—any kind that is in good taste, big enough, and not too heavy. Heavy shoes on a stout woman interfere with lightness of movement—a characteristic for which you must continually strive.

Unless you have very attractive, well-proportioned feet, do not attempt to decorate the bottom of your dress, for it will not only shorten you but will call attention to your feet. If they are very small, they make the body appear larger and if the ankles are large they give an undesirable heaviness, so the very best way, in any event, is not to call attention to them.

Many authorities say that sheer black stockings are the very best for a stout woman to wear, for heavy black or dark-colored stockings are conspicuous,

and light stockings are taboo because they break the height and interfere with the straight-line effect. So choose sheer stockings, and don't hesitate to buy "out sizes" if you need them. If they are big enough over the knees, they will fit better around the ankles. Some big women actually refuse to buy "out-size" stockings because they are ashamed to go in and ask for them, while some medium-slender women buy them because they think they last longer. So pretend that you are medium-slender and buy them if they are more comfortable.

POINTS IN CUTTING AND FITTING
HELPFULNESS OF DARTS

There are many skilful tricks in dressmaking that are advantageous to the overweight figure, as shown in Fig. 57. For instance, the shoulder dart in the figure at the left allows ease over the bust, makes a more comfortable shoulder, and permits of a close-fitting sleeve. It also prevents sagging of the dress at the under arm, giving a neat, good-fitting effect. Don't avoid or "detest" darts; learn to use them so that you get the greatest possible advantage from them. Watch an adept dressmaker smooth the material around and slip out the dart in a line over the bust so that it fits smoothly and easily. Only carelessly fitted and stitched darts are unattractive.

The crosswise armhole dart, as in the upper center, has its advantages, but is not good for a broad-shouldered or short figure, as it widens the shoulder and cuts the height, unless it is wisely made on a bias grain to slant down so that a crosswise line is avoided.

The under-arm dart, as in the figure at the right, is often used with a shoulder dart, especially for very full busts. This helps to shape the material over the bust easily and to give a smooth, straight under-arm seam. Sometimes a dart is used on the back seam as well as the front in cases where the back is fat and round. In any event, fit your dress so that the under-arm seam does not drag, and so that the crosswise grain of the material is parallel with the belt line.

The hip dart shown in this figure helps to fit the skirt by providing a means of lifting the fabric at the sides. If the hips are such as do not curve to any extent, only a slight dart, if any, is necessary. But for large figures, a hip dart is desirable, especially for one-piece dresses. It should be brought up so that the skirt hangs evenly all the way around the bottom. Arrange the dart so that it comes directly over the hip or under the narrow belt or waist-line trimming. Remember that the larger the hip, the longer the dart and the greater the necessity for accurate fitting.

HOLDING UP DRESS ON SHOULDERS

If the back is fat and rounding and the neck fairly small, it is advisable, in order to hold the dress well up on the shoulders, to run a gathering thread across the back neck line. The fulness thus retained may be eased in and shrunken out, if wool is used, so that no gathers are visible but a comfortable neck is secured. Such fulness is not at all objectionable in silk or cotton fabrics, as shown at the lower center in Fig. 57.

THE LONG UNDER ARM

In your quest for becoming clothes, you may be fascinated by the long under-arm line, feeling sure that if you could evidence such a constructive detail, you could look 20 pounds lighter right away.

To achieve this, consider again what you have learned about the corset, its size and its fit. Be sure that your corset has enough supporters to hold it securely down. A corset that "rides up" or a brassière that is too short will definitely prevent a long, easy under-arm line.

Be sure, when your dresses are fitted, that the crosswise grain of the cloth is parallel with the waist line, and that your waist-line trim or belt is placed as low as your dress length will allow—not low enough to make you look top heavy, but low enough for your height, size, and type. To find what this is, walk up and down in front of your mirror with belts, bands, or sashes hung around your waist, one at a time, of course, until you know which one is placed best for you. Don't be faddish nor extreme, but be modish. There is a difference. Work for becomingness so that the line you finally decide upon will surely be right.

THE BIAS CENTER FRONT

Cutting the center front on the bias may give a "silent" or a pronounced line, depending on whether plain or striped material is used. It takes a third more material to cut a dress on the bias, but since it is possible to develop a very smart dress this way it is often worth considering. It should be worn only by the type that can wear extreme things well, however, for a dress cut on the bias is in no wise conservative.

ADDING FULNESS WITHOUT FLARE

To allow fulness in walking, two plaits may be placed in the skirt at the left-side seam, one directly over the other, the right side of the skirt being finished plain. This does not interfere with the slim line effect, yet it gives the desired freedom. Plaitings or

panels of self-color that are 5 inches or less in width soften the line of a dress and, if effectively used, can improve the garment both in line and attractiveness, especially for the figure that is large above the waist. An effective use of skirt plaiting can aid greatly in balancing the proportion.

If the waist measure is large, keep the skirt as straight and narrow as fashion will allow, and watch your sleeves to fit them close and plain. Short, full sleeves and a full skirt must have a small, short waist

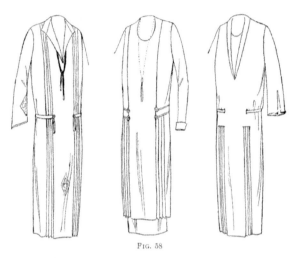

Fig. 58

line to be effective; and all are totally "out of the picture" where the waist and hips are large.

Plaits aid in line and are youthful, as illustrated in Fig. 58, but if fashion decrees straight skirts stitch or press them down straight and slim, for flared-out plaits are treacherous for those who would be slender. For the same reason, you must avoid panels that flirt out as you walk.

A corded girdle, sash, or string sash that is long and limp is becoming.

Tunics, if not too full and if not definitely trimmed at the bottom edge, are advantageous. They slenderize by making it possible to draw the skirt in at the bottom, thus giving an appearance of height. This, of course, is lost if the tunic or the lower skirt is too full. Large figures should always have tunics and foundations of the same color and material so as not to break the height.

DESIGNING FOR THE SLENDER FIGURE

It Is in the Subtle Handling of Details
That the Slender Woman Achieves Perfection

IMPORTANCE OF CONCEALMENT

ALTHOUGH the dress problems of the slender woman are neither so burdensome nor so difficult to solve as those of the overweight type, there are many details which, if properly thought out, can add much to the appearance of the slim figure.

It is true that the use of lengthening lines in a dress for the woman of 34 bust or under does not result so disastrously as do crosswise lines on the plump type, but, at the same time, it is just as important that the angles of the slender woman be concealed as it is that the absence of them be not emphasized when one's weight is in excess of the average. And charming are the means of concealment, for what feminine heart does not delight in frills and color and lustrous fabrics? The slender woman may use all three, as well as many other equally alluring details.

CONCEALING HOLLOWS IN THE THROAT

The High Collar.—The selection of the proper neck-line finish is important, for it will help not only the appearance of the neck itself but that of the face and very often of the figure just below the collar. A rather severe style, but one that conceals the thin throat, is the high collar, one type of which is shown in Fig. 59 (*a*). This can be very smart if attached to the proper dress or blouse design.

If your neck is long, there is no better style to follow for dresses and blouses intended for informal daytime wear in cool weather. Such a finish requires a firm fabric for successful results, so do not attempt to make a high collar of sheer material that will stretch or pull. The elderly woman will find a jabot of lace, plaited or gathered, as at (*b*) and (*c*), a flattering addition to such a collar. For mannish blouses, suited for wear with a tailored suit or a sports skirt and sweater,

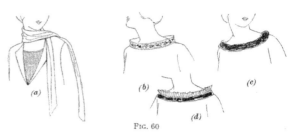

Fig. 60

a high collar is both practical and satisfactory, while for cloth and silk dresses of the heavier weaves, it provides an unusually effective finish, provided, of course, the face is not too thin. When the face is very narrow, it is safer to choose a draped or frilled collar that does not fit so close to the neck.

With a tailored blouse having a high collar, plan to wear a tie of a tone that will emphasize the color of your eyes or provide an accenting note for the remainder of the costume. With the more formal outfit, wear a string of beads just long enough to encircle the throat at its base, outside the collar. This will give a youthful note to what might otherwise appear a mature style. A narrow turn-over at the top of such a severe collar will help to relieve the plainness of the neck finish.

The Guimpe.—If it seems necessary to have the softness of a roll collar and at the same time a support for sagging cords and muscles, a guimpe may be worn. Cut the guimpe from fine net and have it fit smoothly over the neck and chest. It is best to cut the net wide enough to reach about 3 inches out on each shoulder and long enough to come to the normal waist line both front and back. Form a hem through which elastic or tape may be run to hold the guimpe securely and smoothly in place.

The position of the closing will depend on your individual preference. The center back is usually chosen, but the closing may be directly in the center front and ornamented by a row of small buttons if such a finish is desired.

The Buster Brown Collar.—For the youthful, too thin figure, the "Buster Brown" type of collar, as shown at (*d*), Fig. 59, and its variations are usually becoming. If the neck is very long, provide a neck band, extending up about 1 inch above the base of the throat, and in this mount the collar. For a short neck, attach the collar directly to the neck line of the blouse or dress. The appropriate accessory for such a collar is a flowing Windsor tie. Provide one in a becoming color and tie it jauntily to express youth.

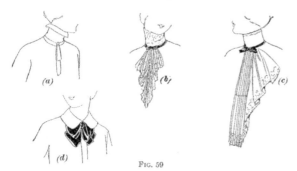

Fig. 59

The Scarf Collar.—Fig. 60 (*a*) illustrates another friendly collar, so cut that there may be a scarf end to throw around to the back. Cut the collar and scarf straight and in one piece and attach the strip just across the back-neck line. Allow one end to hang down in front and drape the other across the front of the garment and over the shoulder, allowing it to hang down the back. Such a collar as this is best used

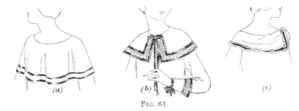

FIG. 61

on a round neck line; in fact, whenever a neck line is cut even a little low, it is wise to have it rounded.

The Bateau Neck.—An oval neck line is difficult to wear when the neck is thin, so most too slim women, desiring to be becomingly dressed, have avoided it. However, you will find that this neck line is not unbecoming if it is built up properly. One means is to provide a narrow stand-up collar, as at (*b*), cut from a fabric with considerable body or made with an interlining so that it will not flatten down when worn. A band of soft, short-haired fur, as at (*c*), provides a softening line, too, or a plaited or shirred ruche, as at (*d*), may be introduced during the season when fur is not a suitable trimming.

The Bertha Collar.—One of the most flattering types for the slim girl is the Bertha collar, illustrated at (*a*) and (*b*), Fig. 61. It not only softens the neck line, but adds width to the shoulders and a becoming fulness to the upper portion of the figure. Cut such a collar from a supple material preferably, although if you are a youthful type, you may use such fabrics as organdie and taffeta. Often, distinctive cuffs, as shown in (*b*), may duplicate the collar in material and trimming.

The Draped Collar.—There are other types of collars that are vastly becoming to the woman or girl who is thin but whose neck bones are not too prominent. She requires a collar that does not conceal but that softens the neck line of the garment and consequently is less trying.

A draped collar lies in folds and has an irregular appearance at its outer edge. The Deauville scarf, as an example of this type, has shown its real worth as an item in dress design by its almost universal popularity. When fads of this or any other kind lose their general appeal, the girl or woman who has found them particularly becoming, need not give them up. Rather, she may adapt them to the newer fashions.

In using such a collar, you will generally find it more satisfactory, as in (*c*), to plan the opening at the side or back rather than directly in front, so that the line across the front of the dress may remain unbroken and in this way prove most efficacious in adding width to the face and figure. Because of the appearance of heaviness, which such a collar may have, experiment carefully on the depth of the neck line, so that the collar will be close enough to the neck for the proper softening effect but still not so close as to appear awkward.

Possibilities in the V-Neck Line.—The tendency of a V-neck line is to emphasize thinness, but it sometimes happens that a design of a dress, although otherwise appropriate, requires a V-neck line in order to bring all the details into harmony. By proper collar arrangements, such as are shown in Fig. 62, it is possible to use such a neck line for the slender figure.

An easy method of counteracting a tendency toward emphasizing thinness is by the use of a frill, about 5 inches wide, of an appropriate fabric. Plait or gather the frill and apply it, having it begin at a point about 2 inches from the right-shoulder seam and extend down toward the waist line, as shown in (*a*). A frill of this type may be worn consistently with gowns of quite formal character or with even a very tailored frock. The elaborately tucked and frilled collar in (*b*) also is effective.

Still another means of achieving the desired effect is to use the material of the dress for the lapels and to make the back-collar portion of a contrasting fabric, as shown in (*c*). Where the lapel ends, join the collar to the dress with some fulness so that the material across the back will lie in folds. Attach two short sections of the same material underneath the lapels to extend toward the center front, arranging these in a knot or small bow. You will find that this line of contrast will break the depth of the V-neck line very effectively.

Evening Neck Lines.—The fact that the neck is thin should not deter you from wearing an evening dress with a low neck line. To counteract the angles of the face and figure, plan for a round neck line, not too deep, and finish the edge with fur or frills of lace. In addition, you may wear a scarf of tulle or chiffon, preferably tulle, or a string of beads. Two or three strands of pearls or similar beads in varying lengths are a most efficient means of concealing hollows in the throat. Always choose such ornaments carefully so that they may harmonize with the rest of the costume.

FIG. 62

33

Fig. 63

ADDING WIDTH THROUGH SHOULDERS AND BUST

Position of the Sleeve.—By the shape and finish of the collar, one may add desirable width through the shoulders and bust, but if the design of the garment requires an unobtrusive neck-line finish, there are many other details of construction which may be introduced to bring about the desired effect.

The feature that probably has most to do with the apparent width of the shoulders is the method of inserting the sleeve in the armhole. It would be a simple matter to plan for fulness across the top of the sleeve and in this way add width, but when Fashion holds the full sleeve in disfavor, you can obtain the same result with the smooth-fitting but more limiting sleeve by placing it in an armhole so planned as to come in exactly the right position on the figure. By bringing the shoulder line well down over the tip of the shoulder, the appearance of width is readily given. The shoulder line that is only slightly longer than normal or even normal will give a good effect. But the short one should always be avoided because it will have a tendency to narrow the figure very unbecomingly.

The sleeve itself should "set" easily in the armhole, which will look best if it does not fit too closely. Ease at this point will give an appearance of fulness without bulkiness, adding decidedly to the general effect of the costume.

The kimono sleeve is ideal for slender figures, so that when it is practicable, this style should be decided on for both dresses and blouses. The effect of such a sleeve is naturally easy under the arm and this is, of course, desirable.

Fulness in Upper Portion of Garment.—Judiciously placed fulness through the upper portion of a garment will provide an attractive and becoming line. By the use of a yoke across the front, which may be an extension of the back-pattern piece, a proper amount of extra material may be introduced in a dress or blouse, as shown in Fig. 63, views (a) and (b). If it seems wise, you may plan dresses of soft fabrics with fulness in both back and front, having the excess material held in place by shirring or smocking, as at (c).

A series of plaits in the front of a blouse, preferably accordion plaits, which have a tendency to open out, is another means of adding width to the figure, while crosswise bands of trimming, placed properly, help too. Always try to apply trimming so that it will produce the effect desired.

Scarfs.—The ever useful scarf, shown at (a) and (b), Fig. 64, is a boon to the slender figure. For evening wear, tulle scarfs are almost a necessity, while for daytime the crêpe weaves in silk, as well as softly-woven wools, are appropriate, the latter as a complement to a sports costume. When the figure is thin, the scarf, unless swathed about the neck, should be worn well out on the shoulders in order to add width to their appearance.

One can wear a scarf in reverse fashion also; that is, across the throat in front with the ends hanging in back, as illustrated at (a). In every such case, the length of the scarf should be in keeping with the proportions of the figure, for its purpose of adding becomingness would be defeated if it were too long.

SLEEVE WIDTHS AND LENGTHS

In dress design, the ultimate aim is beauty, so one who plans clothes must take into consideration the value of concealment. If the arms are beautiful and not too large, as is usually true of the youthful slender

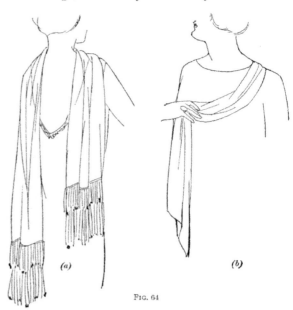

Fig. 64

type, by all means wear short sleeves or dispense with sleeves altogether. If they are thin and straight, make their lack of charm less obvious by covering them, but do so in a way that will be correct for the type of garment and becoming to the figure.

If the shoulder is pointed and unattractive, plan for an elongation of the shoulder line so that the fabric of the dress will be brought down over the arm far enough to conceal the point at which the arm joins the body.

This plan may be followed even in the case of evening frocks, the edge of the armhole where it is brought down over the arm being attractively trimmed if desired; or, if one wishes, a short sleeve, cut from lace, may be inserted into a normal armhole. The patterned

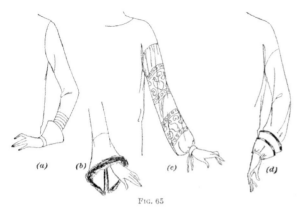

(a)   (b)   (c)   (d)

FIG. 65

effect of the lace will prove becoming and will provide the proper concealment.

It will be found, however, that even when sleeveless dresses or those with very short sleeves are in vogue for daytime wear, there are also certain other types vastly becoming to the slender woman, as shown in Fig. 65. A flared effect at the bottom produced by a cuff, turned either up, as in (a), or down, as in (b), helps to accentuate width even in a close-fitting sleeve.

When a fitted sleeve is required, be very careful not to draw it in too close to the arm. If the design of the dress and the trimming applied to it allows, apply crosswise rows of braid, ribbon, or tucks in order to take away from the severity of such a sleeve.

A sheer fabric, such as Georgette, chiffon, or batiste, cut full and trimmed to produce the peasant sleeve shown in view (c), is distinctive and most becoming. A modification of this type is shown in view (d). Still another attractive type of sleeve for the slender woman is the one that flares out gradually to a point somewhat below the elbow and is completed by an undersleeve of contrasting material. This is, of course, appropriate for only certain fabrics.

Sleeves of Georgette and similar fabrics are very effective when plaited their entire length and drawn in by a narrow cuff.

When the waist measure is conspicuously small, a flared sleeve, which stops just opposite the waist line, is advantageous, especially when the lower edge is finished by a cuff or a trimming band of some sort. In fact, the length provides a means of adding width at various points of the figure. It is best to have the sleeve flare somewhat, but when this is not practical, the design of the cuff may be such as to provide the width needed. A judiciously placed band of trimming will serve a similar purpose.

Value of Cuffs.—For the slender figure, it is well to use a cuff of some sort on practically all sleeves, for such a finish provides a definite line that takes away from the apparent length of the arm and adds to its apparent width, two worth-while features. When possible, cut the cuff from a firm fabric so that there will be no tendency to drag or droop, as such an effect

will naturally take away from the appearance sought. Ruches, plaited frills, bands of fur, and heavy embroidery, all have their place as sleeve finishes, and with the tailored, flared cuff of piqué or linen, provide a list of decorative features from which the slender woman may draw.

LOCATION OF THE WAIST LINE

It should be the wish of every woman to plan her clothes so that they conform in their essentials to the prevailing fashion. In order to be becomingly dressed, however, it is also necessary that the style of the moment be adapted to the personality and figure of the wearer. This is especially true in the case of the exceptional figure, the one that is too slender or too rounded, as well as the too-short or the too-tall types. In designing clothes for any of these types, give thought to the various points of the figure and the means available for bringing out the best features and concealing the worst ones.

Because the waist line is a natural point of division on the figure and because its location on a dress very often has but little connection with its position on the human form, the effect of various locations should be carefully studied and thoroughly understood.

A high waist line gives a youthful air and, when in vogue, may be worn becomingly by the long-waisted figure. The finish required for such a waist line usually causes fulness above and below it, and, therefore, has a tendency toward adding fulness to the bust. Even though a raised waist line may be suitable for your figure in every respect, do not plan for such a style unless it can be considered smart. As a concession to becomingness, however, it is permissible, if desired, to place the waist line somewhat higher than the fashionable position.

The normal waist line is one of the most difficult to wear unless the belt is loose enough not to draw the dress in at the waist. A finish applied just at the beginning of the hips is generally best. Always keep in mind the necessity of retaining between armhole and bust the easy line that was planned for in inserting the sleeves. This is essential for a good effect, for it gives an impression of width and an appearance of fulness, which is very desirable.

The low waist line has many advantages, for by means of it one can bring about an effect of balance as well as provide an interesting division of the figure. The fact that the waist portion of the garment hangs straight or bloused rather than being drawn in, is another advantage of the low waist line.

WAIST-LINE FINISHES

The type of finish used at the waist line of a dress can mar what might otherwise be a smart and becoming style, so considerable thought must be given to the design of the belt or girdle. It must be appro-

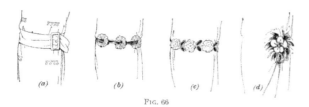

FIG. 66

priate for the style of the dress and at the same time conspicuous enough to provide a definite division of the figure at the point at which it is placed.

In the softer fabrics, a draped girdle is effective, since it is usually wide and is applied loosely, the two points to be sought in all girdle arrangements for the slender figure. If a straight belt is to be worn, have it rather wide, the wide leather belt, as shown at (a), Fig. 66, being especially becoming. The use of contrasting color for such accessories is effective. A ribbon girdle of plaited wheels of self-fabric, as at (b), or of embroidery, beaded, or similar trimming, is always more becoming than a simpler type, provided, of course, the design of the dress permits its use.

For evening wear, the waist line may be finished by a row of flowers applied flat to the dress and interspersed with several leaves, as illustrated at (c). An ornament formed of flowers and feathers at the waist line, as at (d), will emphasize a closing or drapery and at the same time add width to the figure, although not quite so effectively as will the finish extending entirely around the waist.

ADDING WIDTH THROUGH HIPS

The appearance of the skirt portion of a garment is largely influenced by the material of which it is made. The slender woman must avoid clinging fabrics except those that evidence a decided luster, such as crêpe-back satin or those that are patterned in figured effects.

There are certain staple fabrics, however, that have a place in the wardrobe of every woman and that, though their effect may be slenderizing, will be found becoming if the proper design is chosen. This is particularly true of the twilled weaves in wool, as well as of linen and the heavier cottons.

In the use of these materials, cartridge plaits are to be recommended, particularly if these are placed so that they come directly at the hip line or just above, for they will give an appearance of desirable width. If the dress is of wash material and such plaits are not practical, introduce several rows of shirring at each side just over the hips and finish the top with a heading. In the dressier materials, tiers, flounces, and drapery, as shown in Fig. 67, are desirable features for the slender woman.

There are no more appropriate materials for evening dresses for the youthful figure than taffeta and tulle, for their very quality expresses the spirit of youth. Their bouffancy, too, makes them complimentary to the too-slender figure.

PROPER SKIRT LENGTH

The length of a skirt has much to do with the becomingness as well as the smartness of a costume, as its influence on the proportions of a garment is most decided.

The short skirt, besides being youthful, has a tendency to lessen height, and consequently is usually better suited to the slender figure than a trailing gown emphasizing points that should be concealed. In fact, the tall, slender woman may have her skirt slightly shorter than Fashion calls for, except when skirts are very short. Then, of course, good taste must guide her, for even though she is slender, she must consider the dignity required of her and must modify the current style in case it emphasizes skirt lengths that are not suited to her years. She will find, however, that she can wear a shorter skirt than a stout woman of corresponding age.

It sometimes happens that a longer skirt is better, especially when the ankles and the lower part of the legs are so thin as to need concealment. When this is the case, break the length of line by judiciously applied trimming at the bottom of the skirt, but guard against any appearance of heaviness.

The material of which a dress is made determines the skirt length to a certain extent, but the design of the dress itself has an even greater influence, a sports costume naturally calling for a shorter skirt than a

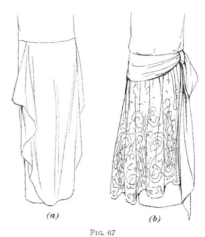

FIG. 67

draped gown, and a suit intended for general wear usually being made shorter than one of elaborate material, cut, and trimming.

Before deciding on skirt lengths, consider becomingness, age, and the suitability of the length of the skirt to both the purpose and the design of the garment. Remember that, all other considerations aside, a shorter skirt is better, but that, when a long skirt is necessary, it may be so trimmed that the effect will be attractive as well as becoming and suitable, for it is the long skirt that holds the balance of power in lending grace and dignity to its wearer.

(a)   (b)

FIG. 68

(a)   (b)

FIG. 69

PROPER SKIRT WIDTH

It is never a good idea for a slender woman to wear extremely narrow skirts except as a foundation for a tunic, for the lack of fulness will exaggerate the slightness of the figure. Of course, when the slender silhouette is in vogue, one would not care to emphasize fulness; but at the same time the idea must be kept in mind that becomingness is of first importance, making it necessary sometimes to add a little to the width of a garment even though this may take away from the distinction of line.

Circular effects in the form of inserts, draperies, or plaits, may often be incorporated in a design to give width while preserving the slim silhouette. Fulness in the form of gathers is often desirable, too, but such fulness is usually best suited to the period gown, characterized by the fitted bodice and bouffant skirt. Of course, gathered fulness at the side seams of a dress is suitable for the more practical gown.

SUMMARY OF DESIGNING DETAILS

In summing up the details of construction just discussed, it will be well to examine carefully Fig. 68, which shows two types of daytime dresses, perfect examples of proper design for the slender figure. Notice the collar, the slightly dropped shoulder line, and the yoke line in view (a). The softness of the plaits adds width, while the crosswise lines of the belt and the trimming bands on the tunic and the lower edge of the skirt, break length of line very well. The flared cuffs are an interesting item.

The use of contrasting materials, as in view (b), is generally advantageous to the slender woman, while the scarf arrangement and the full sleeves add width.

In Fig. 69 are illustrated two evening frocks of correct design for this type. The bouffancy of the tulle in view (a) provides the needed width in the skirt, while the small draperies from the shoulders give a desirable fulness through the upper portion of the garment. A tulle scarf might complete the costume.

View (b) is more conservative, and with longer sleeves would be appropriate for the slender, mature type. Notice the many crosswise lines formed by the deep yoke and the drapery. Clusters of ostrich forming a wide band at the lower edge of the skirt add to the suitability of this style for the slender woman.

If you are of the too slender type of figure:

Strive for the irregular line.

Avoid severity.

Work for the correct neck-line finish.

Avoid drooping trimming.

Avoid any heavy-appearing decorative effects.

Add width to the figure by proper sleeve designing.

Emphasize the loose-fitting under-arm line.

Plan for judiciously placed fulness in the upper portion of a garment.

Select with care the location of the waist line and the waist-line finish.

Consider the advantages of plaits or shirring over the hips and of tiers, flounces, and drapery.

In determining the length of the skirt, consider age, suitability, and becomingness.

Strive for an appearance of easy grace.

VARYING FASHION DESIGNS FOR YOUR TYPE

Producing Individually Becoming Styles by Changing and Eliminating Undesirable Features in Design

TO see a lovely frock in a fashion magazine and then to see this same frock as "plainly clothed" as it is on the pattern envelope gives one an idea of how different a design can appear. This change is often so evident that people are confused and feel that they haven't the right pattern because the foundation usually emphasizes only the dividing lines of the garment.

As you look through books of fashion, do so discriminately, always recognizing the silhouette of a garment and dissociating it from the various details that, however much they alter its character, do not change it in its essentials.

(a)   Fig. 70   (b)

(a)   Fig. 71   (b)

(a)   Fig. 72   (b)

It is only a step, then, to the elimination of undesirable features and the substitution of details that produce an individually becoming effect. Your study of types and of the features that are becoming to each has given you a basis for this work and will help you to see the reason back of every suggested change of line in the models that follow.

TYPES OF FIGURES

Broad-Shouldered Type.—Suppose that you have chosen the design shown in Fig. 70 (a), that you are rather broad-shouldered, and that the drop shoulder is not, therefore, quite becoming to you, a set-in sleeve being a better variety. Also, as your neck is short and heavy, the bateau neck line had better be changed to a V, and you would prefer a simpler dress with a more tailored finish. You, therefore, make the desired changes, and the gown will appear as in view (b). Here, the silhouette remains the same, but the side sections of the skirt are cartridge-plaited, giving a tailored finish, the fur is omitted from the bottom of the skirt and the cuffs, the sleeves are set in and have a pointed finish to give length, and a V neck with a collar is adopted.

Type with a Full, Round Face.—You may wish a simple silk dress, somewhat similar to the one shown in Fig. 71 (a), but you may have a round, full face and short neck and, therefore, know that a V-neck line, as in view (b), is more becoming. You may not be very tall and would prefer not to have your waist line emphasized or your height broken by crosswise

Fig. 73

narrow belt for the sash, and plain set-in, close-fitting sleeves for the sleeves shown in view (a), thereby retaining the principal lines of the dress but altering them for your particular type.

Short, Well-Proportioned Figure.—Again, for sake of illustration, suppose that the dress in Fig. 73 (a)

(a) Fig. 74 (b)

(a) Fig. 75 (b)

lines of trimming. The wide belt may, therefore, be changed to a narrow one and the fur may be omitted from the bottom of the panels.

Large, Round Figure.—Suppose that you somewhat resemble the large, round figure, illustrated in Fig. 32, and have taken a fancy to the dress in Fig. 72 (a), but realize that a square neck line would be more becoming to you than a round one and that the sash, frill, and full sleeves do not give you quite the right silhouette. You can readily change these, as shown in view (b), by substituting a band of embroidery for the frill, a meets your needs for a simple afternoon frock, but as you are the type of figure shown in Fig. 14, the short, well-proportioned type, you feel that a narrow belt, as in view (b), would be better for you as it would not divide your height quite so definitely. You also appreciate the fact that close-fitting sleeves will give you a longer line than those that flare out in bell shape, as in (a). As you are short, proportions will

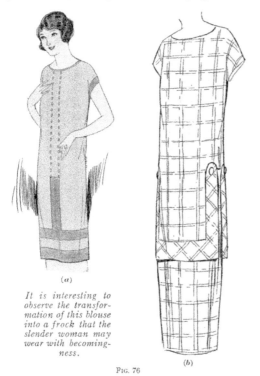

(a)

It is interesting to observe the transformation of this blouse into a frock that the slender woman may wear with becomingness.

(b)

Fig. 76

be better preserved, too, by shortening the line of the collar. And so you change the original design to the one shown in view (b).

Short, Round Type.—If you were like Fig. 35, the short round type, the shoulders in Fig. 74 (a) would have to be changed and set-in sleeves, as in view (b), used instead of the drop shoulder. You will observe that the sleeves in view (b) have a slight flare at the bottom, but this is preferable to the puffed sleeve. Of course, for an extremely stout figure, a tight sleeve would be even better. The V line of trimming in view (a) is a good feature, but it is even more effective in the collar arrangement used in (b). The use of a seam line running down to the godets in the skirt emphasizes height.

Ideal, Youthful Type.—If you are the ideal youthful type that can wear the dress illustrated in Fig. 75 (a), but would prefer something simpler for daytime wear, note the model in view (b). Although the lines of this dress are the same as those of (a), its character is changed entirely by the omission of the fur, the substitution of the trimming bands, and the

(a)   Fig. 77   (b)

addition of a collar. The effect of a plain front panel with plain gathered sides is more in keeping, too, with such a gown.

Tall, Slender Woman.—There are many points in favor of the blouse in Fig. 76 (a) for the tall, slender type, shown in Fig. 23, but, of course, its up-and-down line of buttons and the vertical band of trimming would never do. Suppose that you would like to develop a dress having the same becoming blouse effect, but giving your figure an appearance of greater width. You can accomplish this partly by the use of a material that has a pronounced and fairly large plaid, as in view (b), or a definite figure. The entire absence of any up-and-down lines of trimming in this model and the rather wide bias band of self-material running across the bottom of the tunic also help to suggest breadth rather than height. A variation might be obtained by using a plain color for the bias band. This would break the height of the figure even more definitely.

Ideal Type With Rather Round Face.—If you possess the ideal type of figure, but have a rather round face, it will be very simple to remodel the gown in Fig. 77 (a) to suit you, practically the only change necessary being from the round-neck line in view (a) to the V-neck line in view (b). By way of variety, the set-in sleeve with a Bishop sleevelet might please you better, a very simple change to make. Also, the tunic might be shortened still further, giving the effect of a Russian blouse.

COLOR IN CLOTHES SELECTION

The Right Use of Color Goes a Long Way
Toward Producing an Attractive Appearance

FACTORS GOVERNING
COLOR CHOICE

RIGHT now, if with your hand mirror you sit down by a well-lighted window and take a good look at yourself, you probably will drop the mirror, face downward, in discouragement. But this is unnecessary. Every woman has a right to express beauty in some form. You may not have perfect features, but you can dress your hair and wear your hats becomingly, and you can have at least a reasonably smooth, fresh-looking skin, because the right diet, exercise, fresh air, and an intelligent use of cosmetics will help us definitely in acquiring it. Then, too, you can help tremendously by choosing colors that are becoming, for they go a very long way toward achieving a right effect.

A woman who does not plan definitely to be as attractive and good to look at as possible, cheats herself and all who know or see her, for each woman must decide for herself whether she will be indifferent or interesting, dowdy or attractive. And there is probably nothing in the realm of dress that yields a greater influence in this respect than proper color selection.

Colors for Types.—Read thoughtfully in *Harmony in Dress* the chapter on color, and find your color type in the charts given at the end of the chapter. The chart is very complete, but your age—your youth, rather—your style quality, your circumstances, your buying ingenuity, or your deft use of cosmetics, may make it possible for you to slip into a more pronounced type than that of your actual color rating. For example, you may transfer from the "auburn brunette" to the "colorful brunette," from the "gray" to the "pink and white" type, from the "pale brunette" to the "clear brunette," or vice versa.

The very nature of a "Titian blonde," whose modesty and simplicity make her truly charming, causes her to select the neutral colors in her color scope, the softest, most delicate. Fortunately for her, with her predilection for neutral tones, nature has provided vivaciousness in coloring, so that a definite color would be wholly out of place for her type.

Influence of Grooming on Color.—What colors you can wear depend somewhat on the care you give your person. Carefully groomed women can wear more definite colors than the less spick-and-span women of the same type; but even when brown is becoming, it cannot be worn in the pronounced tones unless one is very careful that the hair is brushed to brightness and the face and neck are at least thoroughly cleansed and talcumed to a point of freshness. It is tragic to see the lovely, brownish tones with shiny noses and ill-cared-for hair and skin.

Carelessly groomed women will find navy blue less critical as a color than almost any other, while the perfectly groomed woman makes navy, in a soft fabric, yield her a full 100 per cent. as a compliment to her care and thoughtfulness.

ADVANTAGES OF A COLOR PLAN

The wisest plan for every woman, except one of unlimited income, is to decide on a certain color scheme and cling to it no matter what temptation there may be to purchase fabrics or trimmings that will conflict in color with coats, dresses, and hats already on hand.

One of the darker colors, such as navy blue, brown, gray, green, or black, should be the foundation color, the choice being the particular one best suited to coloring, size, and needs. To supplement this color, one or two others may be chosen, which harmonize with the foundation color and at the same time relieve monotony.

Brown.—Let us say that you have decided on brown as your foundation color. In such case, complete your winter street outfit, consisting, as it may, of a coat or a two- or three-piece suit, with hose, shoes, gloves, and a hat of the proper color. Decide on brown for your extra dress, but for the trimming choose one of the other colors that you like to wear but that will harmonize with brown. Green is lovely with brown, as are also the rust shades and all the tones of tan through beige to cocoa.

As warmer weather comes and brown seems wintry and heavy, lighten the effect by using tan for a foundation color, shading into yellow as summer approaches. Green is cool and effective for summer, too, and will look well with your tan accessories. Of course, there is necessity for much less vigilance in choice of color for summer apparel because the abundance of color out-of-doors tends to subdue any undue brilliancy in clothing. Then, too, in summer the dress is usually considered alone and is not so dependent on hat or wrap for its effect.

When there is need for more than one evening dress, it is practical to plan a definite scheme for use under artificial light, having the colors entirely different from those used in the daytime, but, of course, equally becoming.

Navy Blue.—If, instead of brown, you should choose navy blue as your foundation color, contrast may be furnished by gray and Copenhagen blue or tan and the rust shades, the blue and rust giving place to turquoise and rose for summer or evening wear. The hose worn with navy blue may be in shades of brown or tan, or may be gray or black, depending on the color chosen for second place. Shoes and slippers may be brown, gray, or black, while hats and gloves should harmonize with the other accessories or provide an accent of color contrast. When it is possible to have more than one hat, choose a brighter shade for one than the other so that the dominant mood may be more readily expressed.

Gray.—The silvery-haired woman of fresh pink-and-white color and the perfect blonde will find gray a fitting background. If you are of either type and your eyes are blue, choose Copenhagen as a secondary color. With brown eyes, rose will be a wiser selection. Imagine how lovely would be a gray Georgette afternoon frock with slippers and hose of a matching shade and a softly plumed hat of rose or blue. If the figure is short, the hat should match the dress, the colors mentioned being introduced merely as trimming.

The shade of gray chosen will depend on use and becomingness. For service, of course, the darker shades are best. When gray is the foundation color, it is not objectionable to plan an entire dress of navy blue which will harmonize most effectively with the gray of coat, hat, and accessories.

Green.—There is a certain type of woman, usually of a lively coloring, who finds dark green an ideal color, its coldness helping to subdue the brilliancy of hair and skin. The use of tan, especially the beaver shades, is to be advised with green, while for warmer weather écru, shading into yellow, is usually becoming. Do not overlook the charm of tan in summer fabrics, as it is most distinctive in sheer weaves as well as in linen and the linen-finished cottons.

Black.—Many women prefer black as the key color in their wardrobes because it is practical, rich, and distinctive, and has the added advantage of being almost always in good style. Because of its appeal on so many points, it is used very generally for street clothes as well as for those of more formal character. Its use is, of course, less limiting than that of any of the colors already mentioned, for it can be worn with practically any color, with the exception of those which nearly approach it. If you care for red and find it becoming, use it with black, or use brilliant green or blue, the orange shades, or deep yellow, employing these bright colors, of course, sparingly. The softer greens, blues, and rust shades are effective in larger quantities, while a still more subdued effect is achieved by combining gray or tan with black.

Even with black, adhere to a special color scheme in the shades or tints you use with it. If your choice lies with red or green or blue, have such color, or a shade that harmonizes with it, predominate in the trimming.

Other Plans.—With these suggestions in mind, work out other plans with the aid of Charts 1 and 2 in your volume, *Harmony in Dress*, making your selection of color with such care that your appearance at all times may be an example of the quiet elegance that should be the aim of every well-dressed woman. You may feel that strict adherence to such suggestions will result in monotony, but such is not the case. Rather, the use of a single color in this way makes for harmony, and there is no more desirable quality in dress design than this.

SIZE AND COLOR SELECTION

In the choice of color as well as line, the ideal figure fares best, for color, by its brilliancy or lack of such quality, increases or decreases size. Because of this, it is necessary to observe certain restrictions when the figure is smaller or larger than the average.

Colors for the Stout Woman.—There are many rules that will aid the stout woman very greatly and very subtly in producing the illusion of slenderness. First, choose colors that recede from, rather than advance toward, the eye. Hold, in the main, to the quiet colors, such as seal brown, midnight blue, bottle green, dull black, blackberry purple, the grays, and the deep tans. These make outlines less definite, help the observer to lose sight of bulk, and thereby make the size of the figure inconspicuous. Besides, they are always smarter than the more conspicuous colors.

King's blue and scarlet and any other colors of their quality, must be "off the stout woman's list" completely, for they definitely create the illusion of bulk. Brilliant, hard, cold colors, or what might be fittingly termed unrelenting or non-retiring colors, should be avoided once a woman is past her first youth; in fact, even the young woman or young girl can't afford to wear such colors, if she is a bit too stout, for the purer the color, the more definite it is to the eye, and, therefore, the larger it makes the wearer seem.

Colors for the Slender Woman.—When a woman's measurements are smaller than the average, she may indulge her desire for light, bright colors and shimmering silk, considering becomingness first, of course. As a color becomes more luminous, its tendency to increase size becomes more noticeable, so that white must receive first place in the wardrobe of the slender woman, with yellow next, then red, and so on down the scale until green and blue are reached. In their most brilliant shades, the latter colors are very conspicuous, but as they approach white they become much less noticeable than the corresponding values of either yellow or red. It is because of this that blue and green are called retiring colors. Considering this, you will realize the necessity for leaning toward the warm, advancing colors, when it is desirable to increase the apparent size of the figure.

Adapting Colors to Becomingness.—In selecting colors, remember that it is possible to adapt practically any one to becomingness. If very brilliant colors seem undesirable for the stout figure, they may be dulled sufficiently by the use of a veiling of neutral-colored chiffon or Georgette, while the dark colors are readily made becoming to the slender woman by brilliant trimming so applied as to relieve severity and break up the surface of the garment to good advantage. Striking color contrasts are attractive on the slender figure.

In making an exception to any rule, special care is required, so that it will be wiser to make use of the safe shades for each type until a thorough knowledge of color and its effect on the individual has been gained by experience. Then you will come to know the joy that a distinctive color combination can bring and the satisfaction to be felt when you have created a proper color background for your personality.

Relation of Color to Age.—In color selection, there is always the necessity of deciding finally about a shade or tint that is in harmony with the years of the woman intending to wear it. Bright colors may be the choice of the young girl provided her type and coloring allow her to wear them, but the brilliant hues must be shunned by the older woman because of their tendency toward accenting lines as well as the slightly faded appearance of skin and eyes that sometimes accompanies the passing of years. It is permissible for the mature type to use brilliant trimming, but even this must be judiciously used, so that her subtle charm will not be overshadowed by the color in her costume.

If you will compare the softening effect of gray hair and the charm of an elderly woman with graying hair with a woman of approximately the same age whose hair has remained its natural color, you will see again the wisdom of Nature and the advantage of copying her plan by graying or neutralizing one's favorite colors as middle age is approached. This will mean the substitution of old rose for coral, of old blue for King's blue, of Lanvin green for jade, and so on through the color chart.

Color and Environment.—As the use to which a garment is to be put affects its design, so does this feature affect the color too. A business girl might choose exactly the same design and material for an office dress as would a girl whose chief concern during the day was amusement and sports, but she would not, as a rule, choose the same color. The tailored frock of the girl in an office must serve a utilitarian purpose and so must be of a serviceable color, while the tailored frock intended for sports wear might be of any becoming shade, frequently the brighter, the better.

The same is true of dress-up clothes. If there is no mode of transportation available but a public conveyance, such as a street car, the color chosen for an afternoon dress should be much less conspicuous than if a motor car is at one's service. Thus it is that color occupies an important place in the scheme of appropriateness.

PROPER CHOICE OF FABRICS

Suiting the Fabric to the Style of Dress and the Type of Figure an Important Requisite

STYLE OF DRESS

THERE is a certain fascination in the mere sight of lengths of uncut material, for our creative instinct yearns to fashion these fabrics into wearable garments, examples of practicability and beauty. In some persons, this feeling is more intense than in others, but wherever it is present, it should be encouraged. Try to acquire the "knack" of visualizing a finished garment, perhaps not in its entirety, but its silhouette at least, so that just the name of a certain fabric will conjure up a picture of it developed into an ideal gown, wrap, or suit.

Organdie, to practically every woman's mind, means a frilly, youthful frock; batiste suggests the daintiness of baby clothes; and serge calls up a picture of tailored things, supplemented possibly by simply cut collar and cuffs of immaculate linen. Of course, many materials are more difficult to visualize in finished garment form than these, but there are certain types of designs particularly appropriate for all of the familiar fabrics. This does not mean that it is impossible to adapt a material to a design, but it is quite true that the results are better when one accepts the limits placed by the weave and texture of the cloth.

TYPES OF FIGURE

The Slender Type.—Along with the importance of suiting the design to the fabric, there is the necessity of suiting the fabric to the type of figure for which the garment is planned. For instance, crispness of weave, as characterized by organdie and taffeta, is particularly becoming to the slender figure.

For the woman of slight proportions, linens will be best in the brighter colors, cut and trimmed to overcome any tendency toward slenderizing. Voile, too, requires careful treatment in making for this type so that crosswise lines receive the proper emphasis.

If a clinging silk is used, a slender person should purchase something with a lustrous weave, such as crêpe satin or velvet, but guard against a color that might have a tendency to make her look "prim."

In the development of woolen fabrics, trimming of braid and tucks will provide the proper break in line for her without taking away from the effect of smart trimness that should be a characteristic of tailored styles.

The Stout Type.—It follows that the fabrics that are suited to the slender woman, must be shunned by the woman whose weight is in excess of the average. This is of vital importance, for the appearance of a stout woman in organdie or taffeta verges on the ridiculous, and its use is, therefore, much more to be censored than the use of a supple material on the slender type.

What fabrics *can* the stout woman wear to create the illusion of slenderness?

In woolens, she can wear all except those having firm, hard-finished weaves, or those with large or definite designs or colors.

If silk is to be purchased, she should consider the closely woven heavy silks. They may cost a little more, but they wear longer; and when one gives thought and time to making a perfect dress, one is happy to have it last as long as it will. Some large women delight in chiffon, Georgette, and lace dresses, but these fabrics must not be used unless a substantial foundation dress is worn under them.

And with regard to foundations, no one needs to use so much care about this feature of dress as the stout woman. It must be wholly non-transparent. It must fit perfectly. And any dress of lace or sheer material fitted over it must follow the slip silhouette easily but perfectly. Some designers use two and three thicknesses as though they were one, saying the heavier foundation softens the line, weights the fabric, and proves altogether advantageous where grace of line is desired.

Remember that materials with a glossy, brilliant surface, or finish, no matter what the color, are difficult to wear and are not generally becoming, because the sheen and, in some instances, the stiffness tend to make the figure appear larger. Materials of soft finish, on the other hand, make the figure appear smaller and attract less attention.

Materials like faille or bengaline, with a definite crosswise grain, are smart and becoming and are best when cut and made crosswise. They hang more limply and, therefore, are more graceful and entirely desirable for slenderizing purposes.

For summer wear, good-quality voiles are better than linens, and the crêpe de Chines are better for stout women than the tub silks because they cling, and this clinging quality, after all, is a vital consideration. Swiss, organdie, or ratiné, like taffeta, are too stiff or bulky to give slenderness, so these fabrics must be admired by the stout woman always from a safe distance. All-over lace is permissible if of small design and heavy enough to hang rather than bulge.

The conspicuousness of large-figured fabrics, big stripes, and plaids makes them inappropriate for the stout woman. Instead, she should choose plain fabrics or those with small, all-over designs. Inconspicuous stripes, however, are desirable.

SHOPPING HINTS

GENERAL SUGGESTIONS

Buy material that is smart and becoming in color; is easy to make up effectively; will give you joy in the wearing.

For economy in cutting, decide on the length you require; then select your fabric so that the width will protect you against waste.

Remember that extra material, $\frac{1}{4}$ to $\frac{1}{2}$ yard, must be purchased if definite plaids or stripes are to be matched.

Plaids require care and skilful workmanship.

Checks are easier to handle than plaids.

Fabrics with design are usually better untrimmed.

Don't buy anything for which you have no definite use.

Remember it is better to get your pattern first and find out exactly how much material to buy; also, the amount of trimming, if any.

Be sure that the design of the pattern is suited to the type of dress that you want.

Note carefully the width of material called for on the pattern. The amount of material required can make considerable difference in the cost of your dress.

Sometimes it is advisable to look through the pattern books to compare similar designs. Oftentimes by omission of panels, ruffles, or tucks, a considerable saving can be made in material; also, a design more to your liking may be found.

The simpler the pattern, the greater the opportunity for individuality, decoration, or ornamentation.

Unless you can have many dresses, don't buy brilliant or hard colors. Then don't do it unless you are truly beautiful—and if you are that, buy the softer, lovelier tones to enhance your possession.

FOR SPRING AND SUMMER

For your summer dress, buy a fabric that will look well after laundering.

Detachable trimmings and ornaments are an advantage in laundering.

In making your selection, remember that wash materials shrink; also that pastel colors are cooler-looking than strong, bright ones.

A sheer dress makes necessary a suitable foundation slip.

FOR FALL AND WINTER

Study wool fabrics, know them, their value, their width, and their use. If you can have only one cloth dress, choose the color carefully.

Fabrics should be good-looking or smart-looking.

Beware of fabrics that "pick" or "fuzz" up.

If woolen materials have not been shrunken, have this done or do it yourself.

54-inch woolens cut to good advantage except in a straight-line dress for a figure larger than 38. Then, because of the need of two lengths, plus sleeves, it is advisable to buy a narrower width, which is always less expensive.

Good-quality wool fabrics cost a good deal, and unless values in remnants are found, it is better to determine before buying the exact amount of material required. For this, a muslin guide pattern is advisable.

Silk fabrics should be richer in color and texture for winter than for summer.

Designs are usually less conspicuous in winter than in summer.

THE HAT AS A PART OF THE COSTUME

The Importance of Considering the Suitability, Becomingness, and Relation of the Hat to the Costume

Fig. 78

THE HAT IN THE SILHOUETTE

THE hat cannot be treated as something complete within itself, but must always be considered in regard to the wearer, her costume, and the occasion. From the standpoint of artistic design, a woman is viewed as a picture, and to produce a pleasing picture the entire costume must be in perfect harmony. The building up, or planning, of such a picture is called costume design. Character and personality, expressed primarily in the face, are usually the center of interest in the picture, while the arrangement of the hair, the wearing apparel, such as hat, coat, suit, dress, fur, shoes, stockings, gloves, and jewelry, constitute the rest of the design.

The costume is judged by the same laws as are paintings and other works of art. Each is a design, involving the relationships of unity, line, and balance. Each possesses texture and color and each conforms to certain laws.

Line and Balance.—The adornment of the head, although not of preëminent importance in the clothing of the body, has, nevertheless, always received a large part of the attention given to dress in general. With the advent of each new season and the corresponding changes in fashion, numerous questions arise about the relativity of the enlarged hat brim to the widened skirt, or of the close-fitting hat to the long, slim gown. In the development of the stylish silhouette, is the size of the hat regulated by the length of the skirt? Is the full skirt really responsible for the greater width in the brim of the hat? And so on.

The answer to such questions is that it is all a matter of line and balance. A unit in design is that to which nothing can be added and from which nothing can be taken without interfering materially with the beauty

and meaning of the whole. A hat is a unit in itself, but when it is worn, it is considered a part of a larger unit, the entire costume; and throughout the costume, proportion must be preserved.

Proportion means the pleasing relation of the parts of an object to each other and to the object as a whole. If a small hat is selected to top off a figure that with every step swirls and eddies with fulness at the bottom, proportion is destroyed. The outline is that of a pyramid, and a pyramidal woman is not pleasing to the eye.

The reversed pyramid is just as offensive, as exemplified by an extremely wide-brimmed hat worn with a knee-length gown. This produces the effect of an overbalanced figure. Proportion in the silhouette must be preserved in order to present a pleasing picture, and the woman whose aim is to be both stylish and charming, must give considerable thought to line, for it is the line of her costume that gives to it that intangible quality called style, as Fig. 78 shows.

To fulfill its mission, that is, to enhance the attractiveness of the wearer, the line of the hat must be in harmony with the general lines of the rest of the costume and it must be well-balanced from every angle. By a well-balanced hat, is meant one in which the weight, or mass of trimming, on one side balances that on the other. For instance, if a hat is trimmed with a heavy mass on one side, there should be a wider brim on the other side to balance it.

The proper placing of spots of color also does much in securing balance, a bright bit of color, which attracts the eye, outweighing a larger mass of trimming. Creating a spot of interest by means of line or color contrast causes the eye to pass quickly from one detail to another until it focuses upon the point where emphasis is desired.

SUITING THE HAT TO THE INDIVIDUAL

Materials.—The texture of material in relation to the individual is the next consideration. Texture is that quality of anything which conveys the idea of how it feels, such as softness, coarseness, stiffness, or hardness.

Texture governs the design of the hat, soft fabrics such as velvet, satins, and crêpes lending themselves admirably to folds and drapes. Select such materials when soft lines are desired as a frame for the face and when the hat is to be worn with a costume of similar texture and line. When severe lines are desired, the heavier or coarser materials are more suitable.

An important point to remember is that not all textures are becoming to all people. For instance, the woman with fine-grained skin, delicate features, fine, silky hair, and a reserved personality will find materials of fine weave, with a suggestion of daintiness and softness, most becoming, while the woman with coarse-grained skin, coarse hair, and large features will find the heavier and more coarsely woven fabrics more suitable and in better harmony with her personality.

Use of Color.—Keen appreciation of color and color combinations in hat selection should be developed and used as a means of enhancing real beauty of face and form by brightening and bringing out character in plain features. Color should charm and delight the observer and blend harmoniously with the personality of the wearer and her surroundings. It should be an expression of the wearer's individuality instead of being worn with a desire to attract attention by reason of its fashionableness.

SUITING THE HAT TO THE FIGURE

General Types of Women.—Although no two persons are exactly alike in appearance, all women who do not need a matron's style of hat might, in a general way and for the sake of study, be divided into four classes; the average, the tall and slender, the stout, and the angular. Each of these types has many variations, so every woman should analyze herself, that is, make a careful study of her physical make-up, in order to know the lines that she can most successfully wear, the texture of material best suited to her, and the colors most becoming to her.

The woman of average size and proportion has no real problem, because two-thirds of the hats designed each season are intended for her. However, the stout figure, especially if she is short, should confine her choice to the hat that will emphasize her height, this being achieved by the shape or the arrangement of the trimming. The tall, slender woman should select a hat that has a tendency to lessen her height, while the angular woman, whether short or tall, should work for softness of effect.

In deciding on a hat, the shape, size, and line should be observed while one is standing before a mirror

large enough to reflect the entire figure. Then the hat may be studied from all angles—direct front, profile, side back, direct back, and side front.

Relation of Hat to Figure.—The diagram shown in Fig. 79 illustrates clearly how the hat may shorten or lengthen a figure. The four vertical lines are the same length and represent the figure, while the added lines on top are those of the hat and represent the effects that may be obtained. The regulation size figure is indicated at (*a*), the straight horizontal line designating the popular types of hats offered each season. The downward lines on *b* have a tendency to reduce the length of the line. The line at *c* appears the longest because the eye is drawn upward by means of the upturned lines. The lines on *d* indicate a hat suitable for the large, well-proportioned woman.

Regardless of fashion, hats are always classified according to this principle; that is, *a* represents the regulation types that may be worn by the average woman; *b*, the mushroom droop, which should be selected by the tall, slender girl who wishes to lessen her height; *c*, the hat that flares up, which should be the choice of the short woman who wishes to appear taller; and *d*, the coronet-line turban, which is especially good for the generously large or broad-shouldered woman. There are many variations and combinations of these definite types, but these four remain fixed.

In looking through a fashion book, classify the models shown according to this principle and then decide which type is best suited to you. Remember that the brim of the hat must balance the figure as seen from the front, the back, and the sides.

The Slender Woman.—The tall, slender woman with a narrow face and long thin neck should avoid vertical and straight lines near the center, such as a high mount in the center front, a crown that comes to a sharp point, or a sharp angle in the trim. Such a hat is built on the principle shown in *c* and makes the slender face

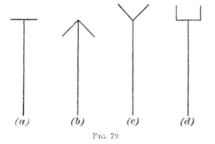

(*a*)   (*b*)   (*c*)   (*d*)

Fig. 79

(*a*)   (*b*)   (*c*)   (*d*)

Fig. 80

look longer. Such a type should select curved lines with horizontal movement and trimming applied at the edge of the brim at one side, for this arrangement emphasizes roundness of features and produces a feeling of width. For her, the large, graceful mushroom droop with medium-low soft crown, shown in views *a* and *b*, Fig. 80, is very practical. You will note this line shortens the distance between the hat and the shoulders and makes the face look wider and rounder.

The Stout Woman.—A large stout woman, with a rather full bust, should avoid a brim extension of greater width at the back than across the front. When this type of woman desires a brimmed model, it should, for perfect proportion, extend out to the bust line in front, and it should be even with the hip line across the back and the shoulders in side width, as shown at *c* and *d*, Fig. 80.

If the face is rather large, this brim may assume a slight droop or a flare at one side. This must be governed by the relation of the head and the neck, as well as line, texture, and color. If the neck is short in proportion to the rest of the body, a straight or flared brim would be the right choice. If the neck is rather long, then the slight droop, but not a decided mushroom, may be selected.

The short, stout woman, with round full face and very short neck, should select a hat designed on vertical lines and having trimming applied at the top of the side crown either in the direct front or at the side back, because this gives an added suggestion of height and causes the eye to travel upward. A woman of this type should avoid horizontal lines and curves that repeat roundness of the face, and trimmings applied on the outside of the brim; also, hats with low, wide crowns and broad, drooping brims, for such hats are built on the principle of *b*, Fig. 79, and have a shortening and broadening effect.

The Angular-Featured Woman.—The woman whose features are angular must use much care and thought in the choice of her hats, for she is usually tall and thin and has sharp features—her nose rather pointed and her chin either boxy or pointed—hollow cheeks, and long, thin neck. To these are often added a stern or severe expression. This type should avoid any suggestion of points or angles in brim line or trimming arrangement, such as quills, pointed bows, etc., because they emphasize the undesirable lines of the face and make the expression appear more severe. Also, a very large hat makes the face appear thin and small and, by deepening the shadows on the face, emphasizes angularity.

Rather, her hat should have a medium-sized brim and a soft crown effect. A slightly drooping brim with a facing of a light, becoming color is especially good, because the reflection of the light and color on the face gives a suggestion of fulness. Soft trimming arrangements, such as ostrich feathers, fur, graceful bows of light-weight ribbon, or crushy drapes of material of soft coloring and texture are good for her.

The texture of fabric is very important for this type, too. She should avoid all stiff silks and satins of high luster, for they will look cold and unfriendly on her. Soft pile fabrics and full, rich crêpes should be the choice of material. Soft material has a tendency to soften the expression; and curves, which repeat roundness of the face, will overcome the angles.

SELECTING A HAT

Taking Thought.—Do you purchase your hats hastily or do you consider your wardrobe before selecting them? Do they express your personality? Do you know the type and size of hat you should wear? Stop a moment and consider these points carefully, for the one great cause of failure in selecting or in making a hat is haste. When you decide you need a hat and rush out and purchase one, you usually buy something that will not supply your needs nor give return for the money spent. Also, when you put off making a hat until a few hours before time to wear it, it generally lacks the finish that shows good workmanship, and, as a result, appears amateurish.

To obtain the best results from money spent for hats, plan well, taking into consideration your particular requirements, your mode of life, and, above all, the gowns and wraps with which your hats are to be worn.

Changes and Variations.—Changes in woman's habits of living, in her dress, and in the arrangement of her hair, bring corresponding changes in the style and size of her hats. Enormous hats, perched on top of a high pompadour, now seem an utter impossibility. But in time, the present-day hat, which fits the head properly and is comfortable as well as smart and becoming, will, in all probability, give place to a distinctly different type, for women will never favor uniformity of dress. They love change and individuality, wherein lies the secret of personality—that quality which makes one human being different from another.

There is no woman so remarkably beautiful that she can wear any style hat; hence, the many variations of every new design. In order to make hats suitable and becoming for all types of women, there may be modifications in the brim line, in the shape or the size of the crown; or there may be variations in the trimming arrangement or in some minor detail, variations that will tend to emphasize the good points of the wearer and draw attention from her poor ones, thus defeating the unkindness of Nature.

Line, Color, and Texture.—To be successful, a hat must be right in line, color, and texture. The line, which is a composite of shape, height, and width, should suit the wearer and be in harmony with the dictates of fashion, for although fashion is not always based on the principles that result in true beauty, no sensible woman wishes to ignore its dictates entirely. The color should enhance the color of the hair, the eyes, and the complexion, and should either harmonize or contrast with the costume. The texture should be selected with regard to the complexion and the hair.

Velvets are soft and rich and warm, but the lustrous satins are to be avoided by the woman whose features are harsh, because they are hard and unbecoming, especially dark satin used without a touch of color or softness in the trimming.

For a dainty, petite person, the line of the hat should be delicate rather than strong and sweeping, and soft pink cheeks should not be overshadowed by hats of intense color.

Blondes, as a rule, look well in delicate colors; brunettes, in the warm, reddish tones; while the in-between types have considerable latitude in the choice of color.

However, line, color, and texture should be chosen not only with consideration to one's physical attributes, but with the idea of creating an influence that will react favorably on the mental condition of the wearer, as well as on the persons with whom she comes into contact. For this reason, consider type and temperament in planning your hats. A dash of color, a becoming line, or a hat worn at a jaunty angle will counteract an effect of overseriousness; bright colors will enliven and make up in a measure for lack of vivaciousness; while it takes a gay, snappy person to wear sombre tones successfully.

Intelligent Buying.—It is not always the woman who spends the most time and money on her wardrobe who is the best dressed and makes the smartest appearance. Rather, it is the woman who does her planning and buying carefully and intelligently, no matter whether her wardrobe is large or small, simple or elaborate. When selecting a hat, consider very carefully its relation to the rest of the wardrobe, because no matter how much beauty it may possess of itself nor how becoming it may be, if it does not fit in as a part of the costume with which it is to be worn, it has failed in its mission.

For the woman whose budget allows two or three hats a season or for the one who is clever enough to make her own, the problem is not difficult. But when only one new hat is permitted each season, much more careful planning is required. In such case, do not select a dressy hat, as this would be inappropriate for street wear, nor a strictly tailored model, for this would be too severe for more dressy occasions. Select a hat, durable not only in style but in material, conservative in every way, and of simple, becoming lines

and quiet colors so that it will be appropriate for all occasions and will harmonize with any costume with which it is to be worn.

Relating the Hat to the Costume.—It is always safe to have the hat and suit, or dress, of the same color. For the sake of variety and interest, however, the hat may be a shade darker or it may be of a bright, contrasting color and of different material. If in the design of the costume, bright spots of color or contrasting colors have been used for decorative purposes, some or all of these may be repeated in the hat. In fact, some feature of the gown or suit should always be repeated in the hat in order to relate it and make it a part of the whole design. This relating of the parts of a costume to each other may be accomplished by means of color, material, or line.

It is from Nature herself that designers have learned to appreciate true beauty. Her ever-changing color harmonies never tire, but you will notice that she uses bright colors sparingly. If you study a plant, you will find it dark near the root, growing brighter and spreading out into glorious bloom as it nears the top. Everything in nature teaches one to look up, and so one plans the hat as the center of interest, the crowning glory of the costume. Needless to say, as such, one must give the most careful attention to its becomingness, its suitability, and the workmanship that is employed on it.

Precautions to be Observed.—In selecting a hat as part of the costume, the following points should be observed by women of all types, regardless of fashion.

Select a crown that follows the shape of the head, that not only fits but that looks as if it fits.

Never allow the brim to extend beyond the shoulder point at the sides and never wear the hat over the face so that the eyes cannot be seen, because the eyes are the most interesting and most beautiful part of the face.

Avoid extreme hats that will call attention to themselves rather than add to the beauty of the wearer.

While much depends on the individuality of the wearer and the style of hat, never allow it to be tipped to one side or to be set on the top of the head in such a way that it seems insecure.

A truly well-dressed woman is never conspicuous nor uncomfortable. It matters not whether she is rich or poor, she may dress with simplicity and appropriateness, selecting her costume to be expressive of her individuality and to be becoming and in harmony with her position in life and with the occasions on which it is to be worn.

SUMMARIES OF DRESS ESSENTIALS

Dealing with Dress Design, Careful Grooming, and the Accessories to the Costume

THE PROBLEM OF MAKING A DRESS DESIGN

THE Journal of Home Economics has published the following interesting and constructive summary of the essentials of a dress design:

The problem of making a dress design involves both technical work and management. The more important part of this problem lies in planning and selection; that is, in making the judgments which precede or underlie the technical work.

The following items are necessary for the solution of the problem: (a) Factors to be considered. (b) Steps to be taken. (c) Essential information. (d) Auxiliary information. (e) General vocational information.

(a) Under factors to be considered, are the following elements by which the success of the finished design may be estimated: Beauty, becomingness, appropriateness, convenience in putting on and off, hygiene, initial cost in time or money, cost of upkeep, and fashion.

(b) The steps in solving the problem are as follows:
1. To consider the individuality of the wearer.
2. To consider the purpose of the dress.
3. To consider materials in relation to 1 and 2.
4. To consider color in relation to 1 and 2.
5. To consider surface pattern.
6. To decide on material.
7. To determine length of dress in relation to good proportion and use.
8. To determine good proportion for length of waist, hem, etc.
9. To select movement of line suitable for the wearer.
10. To consider structure of dress and openings.
11. To determine shape, size, and length of sleeves.
12. To determine shape of neck and collar.
13. To consider place, amount, kind, and color of decoration.
14. To decide on decoration.
15. To consider fashion.
16. To decide on design which is most beautiful, suitable, and becoming.

(c) Under essential information come:

Textile information, including knowledge of fabrics and their qualities in relation to protection, weight, durability, etc.; also their working qualities, and their suitability for the given purpose.

Clothing information, including knowledge of construction and structural lines of garment; essentials of prevailing fashion; difficulties in care and cleaning; and economic considerations such as cost of materials in relation to wearing qualities and reasonable expenditure for dresses of given type and for the particular dress.

Mathematics, to determine the amount of material required and to figure costs.

Art information adequate for the application of the fundamental principles of design. This implies ability to recognize a well-proportioned figure, to adjust and improve the apparent proportions of a poorly proportioned figure, to see and use line effectively, to select beautiful and suitable materials and decorations, to see the coloring of the wearer and the effects of color upon it; to use color in costume harmoniously and effectively; to understand what is becoming and appropriate in costume, and to visualize the finished product.

(d) Auxiliary information includes a knowledge of special terms, such as names of fabrics and terms used in garment construction, in design, and in color study. It also includes the ability to recognize the principles of design in dress, color effects and harmonies, and the qualities of various fabrics.

(e) General vocational information is supposed to give greater general intelligence and to explain the whys of the essential information. In a course for home makers, it might include the science of color and the history of costume.

As brought out here, the essentials for successfully making a dress are technique and good management, including good judgment as to planning and selection.

To systematize your own work in dress designing, planning, and constructing, consider carefully the points mentioned. They will help you to better order, better management, and more accurate results.

FUNDAMENTAL RULES FOR THE WELL-DRESSED WOMAN

Aim always to be refreshingly clean and carefully groomed.

Be slim by being trim; be attractive by being immaculate.

Wear neat, good-looking, perfect-fitting shoes, and trim stockings.

Be sure your corset is right for you, that it surrounds you comfortably but does not mold nor hold the flesh. Let the brassière fit as perfectly.

Have your slip fit without a wrinkle. Have it of the same color as your dress and the depth of the hem shorter.

For your dress, consider what is becoming to you as an individual. If you are not sure, study and experiment until you find what you can and cannot wear.

When you know what is becoming, try to achieve becomingness in an attractive way, emphasizing as much smartness and extreme neatness in dress as age, circumstances, and occasion will allow.

For surety, make a definite rule to assemble your attire and decide on every detail before you start to dress.

When you are dressed, look yourself over carefully in front of your mirror and improve every detail as much as possible. Before the last look or the last dab of powder, consider whether you are overdressed and whether all accessories go together, and especially make certain that you are not overtrimmed with jewelry. Almost every woman improves her appearance by omission rather than addition.

Then, when all is done, put on a smile that expresses the finest that is in you, that compliments you for doing your best. And if, to this smile, you add all the kindliness that you can command, all the happiness that you can summon, your friends and your very own folks will declare you charming.

CHART FOR YOUR GUIDANCE

Now that you have studied the preceding pages and are familiar with *Harmony in Dress*, you can approach a new gown with considerably more security and confidence, having come to some definite conclusion regarding your own type and what are the essentials in correct dress for you. You know what you like, and with the information you have acquired, you should be able to have what you like and at the same time have it always becoming and suitable. "Stop, look, and listen" is good advice in acquiring the sixth sense, which is good taste in dress and which makes for perfection.

To concentrate on yourself the information you have gained, fill out the following, writing down your type, coloring, and points for which to work.

This will help you more than you realize, for you will be obliged to make definite decisions, and decisions always mean progress.

From this study, I find my color type to be _____.
My size type is _____

I believe, after a close analysis, that I should work to express _____ and to encourage a more definite evidence of _____ (see pages 5, 6, and 7).

In the selection of dress designs for myself, I must first consider _____ (see pages 12 to 24, inclusive).
Because

Because

Because

The most becoming neck line for me is _____ .
Because

The type of sleeve that will usually prove best for me is _____ .
Because

The best location for my *waist line* is _____.
Because

The most becoming *skirt length* for me is _____.
Because

Of the modern styles, _____ should prove best for me.
For I should work for line that will _____.
In the selection of hats:
The most becoming in *color* for me is _____.
The most suitable *shape* for me is _____.
The best *size* is _____.

In designing clothes for others, also be guided by this plan. You can mentally note both the good and the poor points of the person for whom the garment is intended, working to enhance the former and to correct or subdue the latter. Above all, be interested in the clothes you make and let your work inspire you to improve, perfect, and make beautiful. Whether it is for yourself or for some one else, work enthusiastically and determinedly to master every point and to evidence beauty instead of commonplaceness.

THE ART OF WEARING CLOTHES

To Be Attractive, One Must Express Good Taste in Clothes
and Accessories and Must Cultivate a Graceful Carriage

ANIMATION AND PRIDE OF OWNERSHIP

THE lovely woman of today has good taste, emphasizes charm, evidences poise. Her clothes express life, joy in the new, and appreciation of the old. Such a woman reads, studies, observes, and knows for herself the smart new, the beautiful old, and what of the two she can wear with charm and distinction.

Sometimes little girls evidence a tendency toward the art of wearing clothes attractively, while others grow up without this ability and as grown women have to cultivate it and work for it. Every mother should help her daughters, as little girls, to wear their clothes nicely, but so often this duty is neglected until children go to school and feel the desire to look like other girls, the urge that is bounded on one side by pride and on the other by humility. Such a girl has a big task

FIG. 81

ahead, but if she tries earnestly, watches carefully, and plans seriously, she can equal any others in the field of dress.

But the planning and making of beautiful clothes will be of no avail unless one wears them well, unless one puts into the wearing of them animation and pride of ownership. If you feel that you are clumsy or awkward in your clothes, exercise, bend, stoop, stretch, and dance. Look over your corsets and improve them if you can. Study attractive women, observe fashion pictures, and then don't copy but adapt and rework. Take from all you see that which

is individually becoming and suited to you; then you will not evidence an air that is annoying or beyond you but will prove attractive and charming in proportion as you study and use effort and skill in adapting fashion designs to your own type.

Never be disinterested in how you look. If not for your own sake, dress up for those who must see you; and wear your clothes with pride and an appreciation of all the fine points that will help to make you attractive. Remember that little details have much to do with the success of a costume.

APPRECIATION OF GOOD TASTE

Every normal woman has an obligation in dress quite as vital as that to dress becomingly, and that is always to dress in good taste. It seems incredible that intelligent women should dress in glaringly poor taste. But we must admit it is true when we see a woman appear at an afternoon, outdoor affair in evening attire, jeweled slippers, and makeup, or at a funeral in a vivid green dress, or marketing in a garden-party frock, or picnicking in lace and ruffles. Make a rule for yourself—a rule that is one of honor for yourself and of loyalty to all other women—to wear appropriate clothes to the best of your ability. Better to buy two gingham frocks than one lace one if gingham frocks are what you need.

If you are invited out, dress to do honor to your hostess, never to embarrass her. If her dinner is informal, don't go in full evening attire. If you are invited out informally for an evening, don't dress as though you were going to a formal ball. Remember that you and every one else will be more at ease where the dress is in full accord with the spirit of the hour. And don't ever offend by overdressing. Simplicity in dress is always to be preferred to gaudiness.

If you find yourself not suitably dressed, try to make amends for it by being as agreeable and happy as you know how rather than utterly miserable. For instance, a woman who had to take a train in an afternoon dress as there was no time to change was most unhappy. She passed through some beautiful country, but failed to see it, made those on the trip with her uncomfortable, and had a thoroughly miserable trip herself, all because she didn't get time to change to a suit or tailored dress. Her last offense was easily greater than her first. So, if, through no fault of yours, your clothes are unsuited to the occasion and you recognize their inappropriateness, help others to forget the fact by disregarding it yourself in so far as you can.

CORRECT ACCESSORIES
SMARTLY WORN

The woman who would dress beautifully must give as much attention to the accessories of her costume as to the costume itself.

No matter how modish a hat is, if it is worn reared back on the head, it cannot be smart or becoming. A purse may be ever so lovely, but if it flops and swings or drops the full arm length at the side, it cannot possess or express style or attractiveness, but rather suggests indifference and a lackadaisical attitude.

A necklace may be ever so beautiful, of just the right color, length, and quality to set off a very chic frock, but if it is toyed with, pulled across the lips, or swung constantly, it fails in its essentials to give length, to provide a becoming neck line, to relieve plainness, or to serve as ornamentation.

A beautiful dress can be spoiled completely by ill-chosen accessories. Wear an afternoon dress of chiffon and lace with a sports felt hat and tailored shoes, carry a service umbrella of drab black and the house-money pocketbook, and your dress will appear tawdry.

Matching costumes to accessories or accessories to costumes should be a law enforced. It is, of course, a definite law in appropriate and artistic dress, but every day we see it abused and broken.

Better to work for one costume complete from hat to shoes, than three mixed ones that do not agree in quality, design, or suitability.

If you have a suit and can have but one pair of shoes for substantial service, then get a cloth dress rather than a silk one. Embroider or ornament the dress or trim it with silk, but work to have it suitable for the kind of shoes you must wear with it.

IMPORTANCE OF PROPER CARRIAGE

So much depends on an erect carriage, and a firm, controlled walk. Beautiful costumes can so easily seem ordinary when shabbily carried. Never slump. Carry yourself with dignity but never with arrogance. Every woman can take on a new beauty, a new charm, if she will practice lightness on her feet, will learn to hold her head well, and will try to use her arms and hands gracefully.

FIG. 82

Fig. 81 gives several suggestions for the woman who sometimes experiences a sense of awkwardness in disposing of her hands. Something to carry, as an umbrella, a purse, a fan, a parasol, or a muff, will frequently relieve this sense of ungainliness.

Five minutes a day given to the practice of standing as tall as possible with the hands in front and the head poised well on the shoulders will aid in the formation of the habit of standing correctly. Such daily exercise reminds one of the necessity for standing, walking, sitting, and gesticulating gracefully. And if, in addition, every time during the day you catch yourself standing awkwardly, or sitting in a slumpy fashion, or carrying your hands unbecomingly, you will straighten up and put your whole body to rights, you will soon

FIG. 83

accustom yourself to the proper attitude and will eventually slip into it without conscious effort.

The slightly exaggerated postures in Fig. 82 indicate very forcefully the evils into which one may fall through carelessness.

At the extreme left is the woman who uses her arms like propellers, thereby destroying all grace of movement.

At her right is the woman who picks her way on feet that hurt. Incidentally, look to your shoes, for grace and ease of motion are impossible when one's feet are tortured.

Don't ever stand with your feet apart or your hands limp at your sides, the third figure from the left illustrating the limp type who looks as though she were ready to drop.

The figure at the extreme right of the illustration also indicates the awkwardness of standing or walking with the feet far apart, the posture here being rendered still more ungainly by the violent swinging of the arms.

Fig. 83 illustrates several erect, easy postures with the feet well placed and the hands gracefully disposed.

At the extreme left is the large woman, one foot

slightly forward, head up, chest up, but not too stiff and soldierly. Notice the position of the hands. The woman of this type, who is inclined to be stout, should make a practice of keeping the hands comfortably in front of her, never resting them on the hips in wash-woman fashion. Such a position broadens the silhouette and gives a "set" look that is most unbecoming. Also, a large woman with her feet apart and her arms hanging like burdens at her sides makes a very heavy, unattractive picture.

Next to the large woman is the average figure in an easy, nonchalant attitude, while at her right is the tall, slender figure in a graceful position, relaxed but not slouching.

At the extreme right is the young miss or small woman with head up and feet placed closely together and squarely on the floor, a very pleasing and suitable pose.

Find your type among those shown and study the posture with the idea of improving your own in grace and charm.

RELATION OF DRESS TO PERSONALITY

Finally, a woman, to dress successfully, must dress with due regard to her personality; and this respect for what is suited to her as an individual must show in her every choice of line, color, and accessory.

There is perhaps only one woman in a thousand who can dare to be extreme in dress, who gains by the sacrifice of the small femininities on the altar of ultra smartness. But with the woman who happens to be of this type, who has the personality to "carry off" the ultra-smart costume with a high hand, so to speak, there must be no compromise. To compromise in the tiniest detail means to fall short of the ideals of her type. For her, there must be no weaknesses, no tiniest clinging to what has once been becoming. She must dare royally with the courage of supreme self-confidence else she fails.

There are many gradations of type, ranging all the way from the ultra smart to the girlishly simple.

There is the type slightly suggesting magnificence with the head well set and the body erect. For her, are regal effects, the splendor of black velvet, perhaps, or the richness of royal purple and deep gold.

Then there is the type of modern all-around woman with an upright, graceful carriage and poised, flexible body, the lines of whose gowns may charmingly express sophistication.

But all along the line, one must take care that one does not slip into a type of dress that is beyond one— that one's clothes do not overshadow one's personality, for this is extremely unflattering.

A style of one's own, not borrowed from any other type, comes with appropriate dressing and means individuality and distinction.

EXAMINATION QUESTIONS

1. What constitutes becoming dress?

2. Describe the Greek law of division and explain its relation to dress.

3. What two illusionary effects are produced by lines?

4. Send us a tracing of a figure corresponding to your type, marked with a dress in a becoming silhouette and with trimming lines indicated, too.

5. (a) What type of neck-line finish is best suited to the stout figure? (b) Name three types of trimming suitable for the stout figure, and three types to be avoided. (c) Describe the use of the under-arm dart for stout figures.

6. (a) How would you plan the neck line of an evening gown for the too-slender figure? (b) What type of sleeve is most becoming to the slender woman? (c) Why is the waist-line finish important when it seems desirable to add width to the figure?

7. Select from a fashion publication a design that pleases you in a general way and tell how you would adapt it in line and trimming to your needs, so that, when changed, it would suit you in every detail.

8. (a) Locate your type as to coloring and tell what color plan you would follow and why. (b) Locate your figure as to type, and tell what materials are best for you.

9. Considering your height, weight, and coloring, what style of hat will, in your opinion, bring out your best points?

10. (a) Sum up the essentials of dress that you are in need of applying to yourself. (b) With a stout neighbor in mind, suggest three constructive points that she could follow to improve line, coloring, and appearance. (c) Consider a slender neighbor or friend and tell the essentials in dress which, correctly expressed, would make her appear more attractive.

CPSIA information can be obtained
at www.ICGtesting.com
Printed in the USA
JSHW031937300421
14042JS00009B/44